A Fork in the Road

My Life in the Nation's Capital,
The Gift and Curse.

George A Owens

E-Book: 978-1-969066-03-0

Paperback: 978-1-969066-04-7

Hardcover: 978-1-969066-05-4

Published by

Columbus Book Publishers
www.columbusbookpublishers.com

Printed in the United States of America

I sat on my bunk gazing into thought, mind bouncing around like a rubber ball with no ending. My thoughts were interrupted by the voice of another condemned inmate, shouting through the tray slot.

"Hey, Reggie! Hey Reggie!" My cellmate jumped off the top bunk and went to the steel cell door responding back through the narrow slot. "What's up! Who's that?"

The excited voice responded "This Ed Slim! Hit some of that Black hole shit!"

Reggie was known for rapping at the Black hole nightclub, the mecca of Gogo on Georgia Ave N.W.

The band Rare Essence kept the Black hole jam pack with DC's finest. They sometimes let Reggie get on stage and represent the Saratoga area in North-East Washington DC.

I remained on my bunk, hand locked behind my head looking around the cell at all the graffiti of names from past condemned souls, who once shared the same thought of hopeless escape. The demon of adversity had a firm grip on our destiny.

"What's next? What's the plan?" I asked myself "Not much at this moment but total darkness, and not a light in sight to guide me through, but hope and faith. We'll figure it out" I told myself, but for right now your greatest weapon is imagination.

The Department of Correction may have your body but don't give them power over your mind. Imagination is your light, I imagine being free until I eventually slipped into the Dream World.

Dedication

In loving memories of my father, Francis G. Winston (1923 - 1996), a true soldier, and my mother, Georgia L. Owens, (1937 - 2016) who has been my strength and umbrella through the worst of storms.

Rest in Peace!

Acknowledgment

Client will provide information for the acknowledgment.

About the Author

I am a native of Washington D.C. I came to Prison when I was only 22 years old, on December 16, 1994. I was convicted of First-Degree Murder, Attempted Murder, carrying a pistol without a license and carrying a pistol during the crime of violence.

I was sentenced to 51 years to life. I remained in prison for decades fighting for my freedom despite being found guilty before a jury of my peers. I was still granted the right of an appeal under DC Code 11-721

My story is unique, but the typical tale of another black youth lost in the system through bad decisions. The Judicial system will show you just how far the rabbit hole goes.

About the Book

This book is nonfiction. The events and experiences detailed herein are true and have been detailed to the best of my recollection.

The names, identities and circumstances have been changed in order to protect the integrity and reputations of various individuals involved, and especially to protect from incriminating various individuals. This book is mainly written to give the reader an understanding, and a clear view of my upbringing and how my life led to this tragic ending.

This book is also written to clear the misconception and stereotype that only a bad childhood could bring about crime and incarceration.

One wrong mistake or bad decision can land you within the stock market of lawyers, Judges, prosecutors and Corporations bidding on your freedom.

Table of Contents

Introduction...i

Chapter 01..1

Chapter 02..4

Chapter 03..7

Chapter 04..16

Chapter 05..19

Chapter 06..27

Chapter 07..31

Chapter 08..40

Chapter 09..47

Chapter 10..57

Chapter 11..63

Chapter 12..66

Chapter 13..71

Chapter 14..78

Chapter 15..82

Chapter 16..91

Chapter 17..105

Chapter 18..111

Chapter 19..128

Chapter 20..141
Chapter 21..158
Chapter 22..170

Introduction

We see it every day, the bling bling on television, and even in the streets. Young African-American men and women drive themselves deeper into the pitfalls of the rat race just to keep up with the latest styles and trends. Young teenage kids doing whatever it takes to be the most fly and most talked about in the schools and neighborhood. African-American people are some of the biggest consumers, spending 300 billion dollars a year on clothes, jewelry, shoes and cars.

African-Americans have come a long way from the days of wearing rags and living in run-down shacks for shelter. Our past has played a tremendous part in our obsession with material wealth as a way of forgetting about past poverty. There's nothing wrong with wanting and possessing the finer things in life but let's not lose everything just to have a lot.

In life, there will be various types of people we'll meet, and one will be more influential in persuading us to take a certain path but it's up to the individual on the choices that are made because we all have a choice. Only you have the power to shape your destiny but on our path in life, we will be faced with a fork in the road and that fork in the road will determine our destiny, this book is on the path I chose and my outcome.

Chapter 01

"The bell rings loudest in your own home."

—Yoruba Proverb

I was born May 6, 1972, in Washington, D.C. the nation's Capital, at D.C. General Hospital.

My mother and father migrated to the District of Columbia from the Deep South.

My father, Francis Gene Winston, was born on March 20, 1923, in Greensville, N.C. He was raised by his grandmother, Martha Winston because his biological parents were abusive. He had four brothers: Walt, John, Sam and Harrell. My father was in the middle. He attended college in Winston Salem, N.C. He joined the military in 1943, serving in World War II, fighting bravely against the Japanese. He went back to college, majoring in political science, and history. He was also very good with Math.

1

He later got married in 1954 to his first wife. Together they had their first child, Debra.

They moved from North Carolina to Washington D.C. in 1955 to find a better life for themselves. My father believed that in order to prosper, a man must be willing to sacrifice. My father and his wife had two more children, Frankie and Lisa. As time went on, their marriage took a turn and they decided to part ways.

My mother, Georgia Lee Powell, born November 14, 1937, in Chester, S.C., was the second to the youngest out of fifteen siblings, Lowge and Sally Powell. Seven of her siblings died early, either by cradle death or as infants. Leaving only two sisters and five brothers. They all worked on a cotton field to pay for shelter.

They worked for a white guy named William Carpenter. My mother met her first husband, and she gave birth to her firstborn, James. They moved to Hartford Connecticut. Later moving to Washington, D.C. My mother's marriage had become abusive, mentally and physically.

Years later my father and mother met and they became involved and she separated from her husband. Shortly afterwards, she became pregnant with me.

A Fork in the Road

Chapter 02

"No one can uproot the tree which God has planted."

—Yoruba Proverb

My father was now working at a laboratory on the Navy base in White Oaks, Maryland, experimenting on underwater missiles. My mother was employed at Harrison Elementary School, as a food service worker.

We were living on Burke Street in Southeast, Washington, D.C. My parents had another child a year later named Natasha.

The 1970s in Washington D.C. was a tumultuous time marked by significant social, political, and economic challenges.

The city grappled with the aftermath of the civil rights movement and the Vietnam War, as well as the Watergate scandal.

The 1960s had left a deep impact on the city, with the riots and unrest following Martin Luther King Jr.'s assassination still fresh in people's minds.

Many neighborhoods, particularly those with predominantly Black populations were struggling with poverty, crime, and a lack of economic opportunities.

Despite these challenges, during the 1970s the city went through a period of revitalization.

The metro subway system, which began construction in the late 1960s, expanded and connected different parts of the city, improving transportation and accessibility. Additionally, it led to efforts to protect and restore many of the city's iconic buildings.

The 1970s in Washington, D.C. was a complex and contradictory period. It was a time of both struggle and progress, marked by challenges and opportunities.

The city's experiences during this decade shaped its future and continue to influence its identity today.

Chapter 03

"Some kids do what you say. Some kids do what you say they do not do but all kids do what you do."

—Yoruba Proverb

The year was 1974, I remember my mother, my brother's girlfriend, her sister and I going to the prison to visit my brother. My brother was sentenced to 30 months at Youth Center Correctional Facility, for Armed Robbery, which was one of the Institutions within the Lorton Prison Complex. He was only 18 years old at the time. He pled guilty to the store robberies.

I can remember walking on a lot of gravel rocks before walking up some metal stairs. We entered these doors and waited inside this huge lobby which was transformed into a visiting area. After 10 minutes of waiting, my brother appeared from behind some burgundy drapes. He hugged my mother, his girlfriend and her sister. Then he knelt down and said a few words to me.

7

I didn't really understand what was going on at the time.

I never understood why he couldn't leave with us. After an hour the guard came over to say that the visit was over.

My brother hugged everyone and left.

In 1976, my brother came home from the Youth Center Correctional Facility. A few days after being released my brother went to visit his father. He found his father dead in the kitchen. At the time my brother found his dad, he had been dead for days due to which Rigor mortis had set in. He died alone from cirrhosis of the liver.

My mother started sending me and my sister Tasha to a babysitter. She lived next door to my mother's old address on Massachusetts Ave. S.E. The babysitter was always drunk.

My sister and I had to wake her up from the couch because it was time for us to eat. She wore a ragged house coat with granny stockings pulled up high. She used to wake from her drunkenness and forget how my sister and I had gotten into her home.

She would ask us "How did you two get in here" until she realizes she was babysitting. When it was time for her to feed us, she would fix us corned beef hash or spam sandwiches, with mayonnaise thick enough to choke a horse.

The toys from her closet were in a big brown paper bag that had dust on them. As children, every little object was a potential toy, because we still have our creative imagination. We lose our creative imagination once we hit puberty.

My sister and I used to go upstairs to our babysitter's room and watch every bus that pulled up in front of the house until our mother arrived on one of the buses.

We were always ready to go home. Eventually, our babysitter's health started failing from her heavy drinking. She passed away also from cirrhosis of the liver.

My mother later needed someone else to watch us. I had started pre-kindergarten at Love Joy Elementary School on 12th & D Street in N.E.

My sister stayed with another babysitter alone while I was in school. I went to school from my uncle's house on Park St. N.E., he was my mother's oldest brother, he lived across

9

the street from my mother's other brother and his family.

The neighborhood was quiet, mixed with whites and blacks. My cousins walked to school with me because we all attended the same school and they were older. The school was located three blocks away. My first day in school was odd because all these other children sat around on the floor playing with these different toys. I can't remember my teacher's name at the time, but I do remember that she was pretty.

In class, we colored, counted to ten and said our Alphabet. Then we started playing with the toys after a few lessons. My teacher had this guy who would come in the class, and teach us how to play the trumpet.

After a few blows, he'd say, "Lesson over! Go Play!"

He would go sit on our teacher's desk, talking in a low tone, what they called grown folks talk. He was putting his Mack down on our teacher. Whatever he was saying, she was soaking it like a sponge.

Then our teacher would holla out "Class over! You all can leave."

Every day, our class would end early when this guy showed up. I had to sit and wait in the cafeteria every day until somebody came to pick me up.

A lot of times I would be in class hoping this clown didn't show up because I knew what time it was. Class over early again!

One day in class, a lot of us were on the floor playing with the wooden blocks that had different shapes. It was these two boys in my class who were hogging a lot of the toys from everyone else. I sat down next to them to play because they had most of the toys between them. One of the boys was light-skinned with a mole over his lip. His friend looked Asian with slanted eyes.

They wouldn't let me play with the toys they had in their area. So, I found five loose blocks against the wall and made the best out of those blocks.

I guess my blocks must've been the missing block to their architect because one of the boys came over and took the only blocks, I had while playing.

This started to be routine each day with these boys taking whatever they saw me playing with.

So, the next day in school, I told myself, I'm not going to let them keep roughing me off. So today, the same two boys came over to take my toys and I just let them do it as if they were getting away with it again. The teacher wasn't paying us any attention because she was entertaining that clown again but she stopped sending us home early because a few parents started complaining. So, I walked right over to them and grabbed my toys back. As soon as the slanted-eyed kid jumped up, I hit him straight in the head with the wooden blocks.

His friend looked shocked when he saw the blood. Then I just started throwing blows to the other kid's face. He balled up into a fetal position until the teacher and her friend broke it up.

That was my last day in that school. I learned pain eliminates the predators. My mother transferred me to Payne Elementary on 15th and C Street S.E.

My older siblings used to go to this school. My mother had enrolled my sister Tasha there too. Her class was around the corner hall.

I asked my mother to stay there with me on the first day of school. She said, "Ok, but let me talk to your teacher in the hallway. Go in there and sit down with the rest of the class."

I kept looking at the classroom door to see if my mother

would walk back through, but it seemed like everybody walked through our classroom door except my mother. So, I thought she must be really talking about something important to my teacher. Then all of a sudden, my teacher came walking into the classroom without my mother. I started crying because I realized she'd left without me. After a day or two I got used to the other kids.

Our teacher started asking for volunteers to be young pilgrims for the school play. So, I volunteered to be a young pilgrim in the Thanksgiving play. We wore pilgrim hats and sang songs while the teacher played the piano. There were about seven of us in the group. My mother came to our play for support.

My mother used to pick us up from school in a gray four-door deuce and a quarter. It felt like we were inside a gray floater. It was very spacious inside, with leather seats.

Our new babysitter, we called her Aunt Martha. We walked to school with her nieces and grandson. They were older than my sister and me. Some days we rode in Aunt Martha's husband's car, he was a short, mild-mannered old man who had a clubfoot with a metal brace attached to it.

He drove us to school mostly during the bad weather

seasons, if he wasn't busy. He drove an old green lemon for a car and he could barely see over the steering wheel. We sat in the back seat scared to death. There were times he had driven out in the intersection while cars were coming because couldn't see that far away, so we helped him navigate crossing the intersection.

Sometimes the car would cut off right in the middle of the intersection. Cars would almost crash into us, while he's trying to get the car started. My sister and I used to be gripping the seats, fearing that he was about to get T-bone but the car would start in the nick of time, barely making it.

A few times the car had cut off in front of the school playground, so embarrassing. We covered our faces with the school books and got out of the car. He eventually passed away.

Before going home our mother sometimes would treat us to Holly Farms Chicken spot and get a two-piece chicken dinner. Other times we would just go home and Ma would cook us dinner before our father arrived from work.

My father usually gets home around 5 o'clock. My father didn't drive any more due to a bad car accident, so he caught a ride with his co-worker.

A Fork in the Road

My father had a pot belly, afro like the Houston Oilers running back Earl Campbell and pork chop sideburns. Once everyone was home then dinner would be served.

Chapter 04

"There is a power greater than myself who loves
me exactly as I am."

—Yoruba Proverb

The year was 1978 when I met one of my first best friends in the neighborhood, named Charlie.

He was the nephew of my brother Frankie, an old running partner. Charlie had a big forehead and sinister smile when we were kids. He was climbing on our gate with his brother Jarvis.

We introduced ourselves and hit it off quickly. He lived a few houses from me. We even went to the same school. I felt good meeting new friends.

I saw Charlie the next day in my new classroom. We both had started the first grade. Our teacher was a religious woman who had prayer sessions in the classroom before doing our work assignments.

Charlie came to school with some blue tough skin jeans, and worker boots, like a construction worker. I hated coming to school with the black book sachet that my father had gotten from work. I didn't want to carry a book sachet as a kid. Inside my sachet was writing paper, some strong-smelling brown glue that could probably glue together a car. I had mechanical pencils, a blueprint ruler, an eraser and other stuff inside that my father got from his job.

My mother had prepared my lunch box. During our lunch recess, I saw Charlie sitting at the lunchroom table with his cousin. I walked over and sat down. I opened my lunch box, pulling out my tuna sandwich, cookies and Sip-up drink. Some more new friends walked over to the table and sat down. Donald lived in the corner house on our block. As a matter of fact, I met Donald before I met Charlie. Donald was a fat light-skinned kid with a birthmark on his cheek. He was very smart and good at math. Him and his little sister were raised by their father, who was big in stature. He seemed to be a very strict man, he always had Donald and his sister doing chores.

Then there was another good friend named Umar, who

came to the table. He had just moved across the alley from us. Umar was light-skinned with a slightly dark brown afro. Umar's family were Muslims. Umar was really smart in class like Donald, always participating in the science projects. He was an only child. I liked going over to Umar's home and playing with the action figures. These were my earliest childhood friends.

Chapter 05

"God makes three requests for his children; Do the best you can, where you are, with what you have, now."

—Yoruba Proverb

The neighborhood we lived in was considered the Capitol Hill area of Washington, D.C. Brick row houses, with two levels and a basement, was the norm in my neighborhood. On the porches, a lot of the residents had plants hanging up with chairs set nicely on their fronts.

In our neighborhood, a lot of the homes were owned by the older generation. The majority of the owners had migrated from the Deep South. We had a mixture of whites and blacks living in our community but the blacks were the majority in our area until one traveled further down Pennsylvania, East Capitol and Constitution Avenue toward the Capitol, that's where the white folks were the majority but in the opposite direction, across the Susa and East Capitol bridges, going into the deep south-east, the area was more populated by the blacks.

In these areas, the crime rates were higher, around Barry Farms, Savannah Terrace, Park Chester, Valley Green, etc.

On our block most of the kids my age were raised by their grandparents. My parents were in the same age range as the other kid's grandparents. Everybody knew each other in the community.

Around the corner on 19th Street was the D.C. Jail. The Jail was used to house guys while awaiting trial, court or their destination after sentencing. Whenever we heard the siren sound coming from the prison it was a signal, alerting the community that someone had escaped but the majority of the time it was just a drill.

One particular day, it was the actual thing. A prisoner had just escaped and the siren sounded off over the neighborhood. My mother, my sister and I were leaving the house through the backyard. As we were walking down the alley, around noon we saw a black male running down the alley behind us. Our mother moved to the side, shielding me and my sister. The guy ran past us, looking exhausted and just as afraid as we were. He didn't know if the police were around the corner, or about to turn up the alley on his tail.

The way our alley was directed, when you exit the alley

behind our house, another street, which was 18th Street, crosses it and then the alley continues until you hit 17th Street but the guy crossed 18th St. heading down the next alley. About a minute later, after the guy had hit the second alley, the police squad car came flying down our alley. The police slowed down and asked my mother if she'd seen a guy running down this alley.

My mother looked at the officer in the squad car with a plain face and said "No!"

The officer said, "Ok, thank you, Ma'am."

The officer proceeded across 18th street, down the other alley in the direction the man had run.

When we got into the car, I asked my mother why she'd told the officer that she hadn't seen anything when she had. My mother looked at me through the rearview mirror while cranking up the car, she said "It's safer to mind your business. You'll live longer."

My sister, who was in the front seat, looked at our mother and said, "Ma, I didn't see anybody."

My mother looked at me through the rearview mirror waiting for my response.

"I didn't see anything either Ma," I said.

Then my mother said, "None of us saw anything."

From that day, I learned to mind my business and...live longer.

In our neighborhood, the people were big on celebrating holidays: Easter, Halloween, Thanksgiving and Christmas. I remember one Easter, my mother sent me to church with my brother Bay. I had to go to church before I could play with my Easter toys, and plastic eggs with little surprises inside them.

On this day, my mother had dressed me in a sky-blue suit and some hard black shoes. I had a big Jackson five afro. I sat on the couch waiting for my brother to arrive. Fifteen minutes later, my brother pulled up in the alley behind the house. My brother was driving a silver 79 Mustang at the time. He got out of his car wearing a brown suit with his collar open like John Travolta on "Saturday Night Fever." He had on some dark shades. I thought my brother was the coolest dude on the planet. He came into the house and asked if I was ready to go. My mother kissed me on the cheek and said, "My baby is ready."

We got in the car and proceeded to church. When my

brother turned on the car, Rick James sounded out through the radio. 'She's a Super Freak!' blared into the Mustang, preparing us for anything but church. I was hoping it took hours to get to church because I didn't want to go but we got there within 15 minutes. I was wondering where the church was then I saw a little building that looked like a clubhouse, with a narrow door that my brother pulled up in front of. We got out and entered the little building.

When we went inside, we walked down some stairs as if headed down the basement of the house. When we got downstairs, there were a lot of people crammed down in a small area, sweating and waving a cardboard fan. The preacher appeared from out of the bathroom wearing a toupee, black robe and gold rings. The chairs we sat on were steel folding chairs. Everybody opened up their bibles as if they knew the scripture he was going to recommend. The preacher asked everybody to bow their heads for prayer. It felt like he was preaching for 30 minutes straight without a pause then his voice rang out into the small area "... and the Lord said unto Satan, hast thou considered my servant Job, that there is none like him..."

In the small crowd, someone screamed out "Preach on!"

I looked over at my brother, who had a bogus look of interest in what this preacher was saying on his face.

My brother still had on his dark shades chewing his gum. I was ready to go home, but tried to imitate my brother by looking serious and interested, but in my young mind, I was saying 'This is some bullshit! Why did Ma send me and not my sister.'

Finally, it was over. When it was over, everybody stood up, embraced and shook hands. The preacher had someone walk around collecting the money for the church tides. When the lady came near me, I faked like I dropped some money in the small tray. We finally got out of there and headed home.

My mother was in the kitchen cooking while my father was in front of the television watching the Easter Day parade. My sister was in her room playing with her dolls. I immediately jumped into playing with my easter toys. I always had it good on holidays. Even when I had lost a tooth, I knew there was a good chance a dollar was going to be under my pillow.

One evening my parents threw a birthday party for me for which I had a few of my friends over. My party had cake, chips, sodas, ice cream and comic books scattered all over the coffee table because my parents knew how much I loved the different

24

Superheroes. There were birthday ornaments, decorated all over the basement because that was our social area. They had Earth, Wind and Fire playing on the record player.

My party turned into a party for the adults. A lot of the kids left and the adults took over. They had bottles of Vodka, Gin and grapefruit juice. Some of the adults had passed out on the couch. My mother and father were dancing, while his friend Bob was sitting at the table singing with the record, slamming down cups of gin until he had passed out.

When it was over, everybody had passed out drunk. When I woke up and came down the stairs everybody was snoring at 3 am, lying all over the couch, kitchen table and even laying on the floor. My mother was lying on the floor sleeping. I had to clean up all the mess myself. I was eight years old. That was one of the reasons I never liked alcohol coming up.

Chapter 06

"In our deepest hour of need, the Creator asks
for no credentials."

—Yoruba Proverb

Coming up as a child, I loved to read. I was in the R.I.F
program (Reading is Fundamental). My favorite books were
about dinosaurs and animals. My library teacher had a huge ass
like a horse. When she walked in the hallway, her dress would
swing from side to side, and her rear end came to the height of
my eyes. We had to read a certain number of books a month
in the R.I.F program. This mold shaped me into becoming a
lover of books. I still carried on reading once I got home,
especially through the encyclopedias. This became my passion,
and enhanced my imagination to be different from the norm.

Charlie and I were also in the same class during the second
grade. He still had on his worker's boots and a different type
of tough-skin jeans. We sneaked and talked in class. I would
do my work, then talk but Charlie would talk, then do his work.
Charlie's silly laugh made it hard not to laugh too. Our second-

grade teacher was no-nonsense. If you got caught, she would make you stand in the corner for hours, so I had to play it cool, hiding behind other classmates, while tripping off Charlie, Antonio and Rick.

Rick lived around the corner from us, on Independence Ave. He was tall, and slim and kept a smile on his face. Rick always kept the latest tennis shoes. Antonio was also tall with big front teeth. He lived near Potomac Gardens, a drug-infested neighborhood. He wasn't as fortunate as some of us. His sister was also in our class. She was the pee girl. She always smelled like piss but she wasn't a bad-looking girl.

In my third-grade year, Charlie didn't pass but in my class was Melbo "aka Touch," he lived on my block. He had stayed back in the 3rd grade.

After school, a lot of us got together and played touch football in the streets or basketball in the alley, with the bicycle rim for a basket.

On my street, we had Charlie, Touch, Leo, Dre "aka Booster," Kenny "aka Chi," Mike "aka Mick," Troy, Mike B, Keith, Chuck and Jarvis. The older teens were Warren "aka Duck," Dave "aka Cheek," Rob "aka bandit," and Carl "aka Caddy."

Our rivals were the boys who lived on 17th and Bay Street. Bay Street was around the corner from us. On their street, it was three times the amount than us. They had a lot of cousins, brothers and sisters, living under one roof like refugees. When they came on our street to play with us in football, it looked like a fight was about to break out, because they had more kids on their team. They came to our street with everybody, even the stray dogs that they found in the alley. On their team were Bob, Mike, Rome, Pork, Joe, Reno, Drizzy, Ed, Bumpy, Fish, and Ed but it was about two dozen cousins and little brothers standing around, leaning on people's cars and sitting on the curb.

After a few plays, a fight broke out between Dre "Booster" on our street and Dre from their street. Before you knew it, everybody was fighting. Everybody that sat on the curb jumped up and started throwing blows, grabbing me and Leo from behind while I was on top of another kid. Even their stray dogs came to the rescue biting Mike and Touch on the leg. Whenever they were losing, somebody on their team always started a fight. The elders on my street broke it up and sent everybody home.

We all saw each other at school the next day and were back to being friends.

Chapter 07

"Don't be afraid to look at your faults."

—Yoruba Proverb

My sister Tasha wasn't too much of a hanging outside type of girl. She was more shy. She hung around our mother a lot but when she did play outside, it was with a limited number of friends. But as for me, I was all over the neighborhood. I had met one of my other best friends named Charles "aka Fiche."

I met Charles through Chi. Charles and Chi used to play together, but Charles stopped playing with Chi because he was stealing Charles's Matchbox cars when he wasn't looking. Chi was always sneaky. He lived with his grandmother and father, Big Kenny up the street from me. Chi was small and skinny, with a push-back hairline. He had a wild household. His grandmother provided him with everything he needed and wanted. He had a basketball court in their backyard, where we used to go play ball sometimes.

Chi's father, Big Kenny, wasn't wrapped too tight mentally. He would sometimes try to play basketball with us, and just break out laughing whenever any of us got injured. I remember one day we were playing "butt on the pole" in which the player with the lowest points after the winner had scored 33 points first, the loser had to face the pole while everybody takes turns throwing the ball at your ass like getting spanked for losing. The majority of the guys throw the ball as hard as they can to make you feel.

On this particular day, I was the lowest-scoring player on the team, and I had to face the pole. There were about five people in line, including Big Kenny. Chi had smeared some berries on the basketball. I was wearing some white jeans. Chi's father threw the ball and smeared berries all over the back of my pants. Everybody broke out laughing. I looked at the back of my pants in the reflection of their door mirror. I wanted to punch Chi's father in the face, but he was a grown man, and too big for me. So, I rushed home and told my mother. Even though my father was home, I saw my mother first. She was cooking, as usual, and I told her. My mother was more aggressive in these situations when it came to her kids. She looked at the back of my pants and went off. She grabbed a butcher knife out of the kitchen drawer and grabbed me by the arm.

"Let's go!" she said.

When we got up the street, Chi and his father were peeping out the front door. My mother had the knife in her house coat pocket, standing in front of their house cursing.

"Bring your black ass out here, cock sucker!" my mother shouted.

She walked up to their porch and started banging on their door. Ms. Montgomery, Chi's grandmother came to the door.

"What's the matter, Mrs. Owens?"

My mother was trying to look over Ms. Montgomery's shoulder into the house to see if she saw Chi's father.

"Your son, Chi's father, put this shit on the back of my son's pants. Look at this shit!"

I was standing there beside my mother breathing hard

because I was ready to fight her grandson. Then my father came up the street and into their yard.

"What happened, George?" my father asked.

"Look at the back of his pants," my mother spit out with rapid fire.

My father looked and I could see my father's facial expression change from rational to irrational.

"Who did this?" my father asked.

I was still breathing hard with anger.

"Chi's father," I said.

"Kenny!" Ms. Montgomery yelled out.

Ms. Montgomery was a rough-looking woman. She was jet black with a knife scar on her arm and a cut across her left eyebrow that broadcast her past street life which had obviously been hell. She used to be a madam in the early 70's, controlling several women. She was a heavy-set woman that walked like an Orangutan in a skirt.

Chi and his father came to the door.

"Did you put these berries on the back of George's Pants? Because if so, you need to apologize." she barked.

A Fork in the Road

Chi tried to play it off like this was new to him. When I saw his facial expression, like he didn't know anything, I immediately tried to go at him. My father held me back, but my mother tried to attack Chi's father. There was a big commotion on their front porch. My mother was breathing hard with her hand on the butcher knife. I was big for my size, and Chi knew he couldn't beat me, so he stayed behind his grandmother. Before it was over, both Chi and his father apologized but I still wanted to at least get even by punching him out.

Chi's father died a few months later from some strange illness. Chi and I started talking again after a few weeks.

Fiche started coming over to the house on his bike. Fiche lived on 18th and Bay Street. The 18th Street side of Bay Street was quiet, there were fewer children our age on that side but the 17th side of Bay Street was alive with kids. Fiche liked to play pretend games like, what if we were the characters on Scooby Doo or The Flintstones.

My parents liked Fiche, but some evenings my parents felt Fiche was coming over too much. Fiche looked at my parents as his own, since he never really had a relationship with his parents. He was being abused by his mother's boyfriend for years. So, we became his family.

I remember the block party days on our street. The block parties were late in the evening around 7 pm, during the summers. You could see everybody on our block decorating the street with party items around the light poles. Mrs. Herman usually sets the tables with food. Charlie's uncles, Jack and Glen would hook up the amps for the speakers. Block parties were one of my favorite moments as a child because I liked seeing everybody getting together and enjoying themselves and the sounds of Donna Summers blasting through my head. The older females walked through the crowd carrying their plates of food, looking like celebrities.

We had some sexy girls in the neighborhood, but they were chasing the other older guys. Bunny, Sugar and Michelle were looking to dance with Tom, Dave and Caddy. All of them were around the same age, in their teens. Then there were some of the other fly girls from around the corner, off Massachusetts Ave, that attended the block party. Vowel lived on Mass. Ave. She had a sister my age named Charlene. Both sisters were gorgeous, with her coffee cream complexion. She also had a nice body and a sexy walk but she also was a Tomboy, especially when it came to drama. She had two brothers, Knuckles and Champ. Both her brothers were boxing for recreation. Champ was the oldest, and Knuckles was around my age, but a few years older. Vowel had some of her friends with her, Tammie, Toya and April. They were also sexy.

On my block were Rhonda, Tonika and Winnie. Rhonda was bi-racial with Caucasians, Indian and Black but the biggest turn-off was her attitude.

Me, Charlie, Keith, Chi, Chuck and Touch. We all sat against the brick stumps, admiring the girls and envying the older guys, who were Mel, Tim, Donny, Earl and Rodney. All these dudes were the popular older teens in our neighborhood, and they were nice with their hands.

My friends and I used to watch these guys come on the scene and get sweated by the girls we were sweating.

"One of these days, those same broads are going to sweat me too," Keith said with a distant look in his eyes.

Keith was an only child. His grandmother kept him on a tight watch. Keith was going to a private school on 15th and A street in S.E. called Holy Comforter. We used to laugh at Keith because he wore a Uniform to school while we all got a chance to wear our regular clothes. Keith was a light brown complexion with wavy hair. He was good with doing wheelies from the beginning of the block to the end of the block.

Chuck looked over at Keith and said, "Man, ain't nobody going to sweat you. If your grandmother even sees you talking to a girl in front of the house, she's going to make you do extra prayer duty."

Everybody started laughing. Chuck was the clown of the group. He always had a grin on his face like he was thinking about something funny. Chuck was short, with a birthmark under his left eye resembling a black eye from fighting. He lived with his mother and two little brothers on Minnesota Ave. N.E., but he would sometimes stay over at his grandparent's house on our block. Chuck's mother worked two jobs, trying to support Chuck and his two brothers.

Everybody who hung together basically got everything they needed from their parents or grandparents. The majority of my childhood friends didn't have their fathers in the household.

Some didn't even have their mothers in the household. We all lived in two-level brick row houses, with a basement. Our families made alright incomes, but we were still considered poor, just a little more fortunate than the other poor kids. When you're a kid with no responsibilities, and your parents provide you with the world, you feel like money grows on trees but it's always good to instill responsibilities in the child early because if not, they'll never know the importance of hard work.

Chapter 08

"If you plant turnips, you will not harvest grapes."

—Yoruba Proverb

As a child, I grew up watching a lot of television programs. My father watched a lot of the old movies, and programs like Jeopardy, which I hated as a child. He was a history buff and information addict. Beside his chair was a stack of educational books. He had every book lined in a certain order in which he knew if someone was looking through his books or even sitting in his chair. My father was a stern man. He believed in working hard and providing for your family. My father came up under strict discipline. He believed that you eat what your family provides. No alternatives.

Our mother pretty much spoiled us, with options of what we wanted to eat and my father didn't like that. He didn't like us drinking juice or Kool-Aid until we were finished eating our meal. He said drinking while eating made you full, and you couldn't finish your meal if you were full which would end up being a waste of food. We had to make sure that we washed our dishes, and cleaned up behind ourselves. Our rooms had to always be straightened up and bed made before leaving out. My father didn't play in that junky room mess.

My sister wasn't as neat as me. She always failed his inspection. These were the few moments I was the one getting fussed out. I liked hanging around my big brothers. My brother Frankie was in college, playing football. He was very athletic. I only got a chance to see him on holidays and during the summers. When he was home during the summer, he usually worked at the Boys and Girls Club on 17th and Mass. Ave. S.E. My brother would sometimes take me up to the school, Payne, on the basketball court and show me some moves. We would practice shots from different angles. My brother was playing basketball in Nebraska State College before later attending Huron South Dakota playing Football. My brother had trophies all through our living room for basketball and Football. The Minnesota Vikings had contacted my brother, but he got injured shortly afterwards, destroying his opportunity. Whenever he was home, the females started blowing our phone line up. He kept a different female over the house in his room. Both my brothers were smooth with the women. Both my brother's weaknesses were Angel Dust and

PCP.

I remember my brother Bay was living alone on Stanton Road S.E. He said that he had started smoking pot early, at age 10 but as he got older, he started experimenting with a more potent type of reefer called Phenyl cyclohexyl piperidine (PCP) also known in its use as angel dust among other names. In the streets, they called it "Love Boat" or "Butt Naked"

One evening my mother gave my brother Bay a ride home from our house. We all went into his apartment, which was on the first floor. These were three-level apartments, with a balcony on the upper levels. The first level only had a little patio, with sliding doors. My mother and I sat on the couch while my brother fumbled around the kitchen. I was about 9 years old.

My brother's phone rang and he answered it, talking rapidly to someone on the other line. When he hung up the phone, he went straight to the bathroom and closed the door. My mother started calling his name because he was in the bathroom for about 45 minutes. When he came out, my mother asked him if everything was okay. He didn't answer but went back to fumbling around the kitchen like he was looking for something. Then all of a sudden, my brother bent over the kitchen table, as if his stomach was aching. My mother asked him if he was having stomach pains. He still didn't say anything. Then he started mumbling something.

"Con cheeta! Con cheeta!! Con Cheeta!!!"

He started getting louder and louder.

"Con cheeta!!!"

Then he just, out of the blue, flipped the table over, sending everything that was on the table flying in the air. My mother jumped back. I stood up, wondering what was wrong with my brother. Then he started hitting the apartment wall, causing dents like he was Superman.

My mother grabbed my coat and said "Put your coat on and let's get the fuck out of here. Your brother has been smoking that shit!"

We exited his apartment and got in the car. While we were in the car pulling out of the parking lot, I could see my brother's silhouette through his curtails throwing objects across his apartment.

I asked my mother "What's wrong with Bay?" She lit up a cigarette and said "He has lost his damn mind that's what's wrong with him!"

43

The year was 1981, and I was in the 4th grade. My teacher was an obese, no-nonsense woman with a gorgeous face. She had a small gap between her teeth. Even though she was heavy set, still she had curves. For some reason, she didn't like me that much, because she recommended, I attend summer school, even with a passing report card. I know that I talked and laughed in class, but I always did my work, and I was in numerous activities.

I was in the Nancy Reagan "Say No to Drugs" for the youth program, The Young Astronaut Club, The Darrel Green youth fitness program, also the Gifted and Talented but when I was recommended for Summer School, I knew my whole summer was going to be trashed. My friend Umar had to attend Summer School too. Umar was a brainy kid, so I knew she was just being vindictive but it was good to have some company and a friend to talk to through this summer school crap. The nearest summer school was Ludlow-Taylor, off 13th and H Street N.E. I had to miss all the fun summer places like the Zoo, Mall, King Dominion, Busch Gardens and the Park. The class they assigned us to was overcrowded.

This class looked like something off "Welcome back Carter." I only saw the teacher once, and that was on our day of enrollment. She dropped off some assignments and we never saw her again. We had students sitting on the radiator and standing up because there weren't enough chairs. There was a brother and sister in our class that looked like they belonged in high school. He had facial hair and she had breasts like a grown woman. They kept an evil look on their face that intimidated the other kids without saying a word.

There were some more rough-looking kids in our class. One morning it was these two boys fighting on the staircase. One was a skinny kid and the other boy was chubby. They fought so long that everybody got tired of watching and went back inside the classroom. There was no teacher on site to break it up. When some of us went to see what happened, one boy was on the steps sitting down with their head in his hands. And the other boy was bent over drinking water at the fountain. Their clothes were torn and bloody. This was the highlight of our boring summer.

The next day I got into it with another kid over a seat. He said let's take it outside after class. I said "Okay, let's take it outside after class"

I could see that a lot of the kids were on his side because they were from the same area in the North East. I only had

Umar, and he looked just as nervous as I did but I played it off with a look of confidence, but my heart was racing. I figure we probably get jumped. I kept looking at the clock. It's almost close to that time. The bell rang, and everybody rushed outside to see a fight. I looked at Umar, he looked at me. We both were the last ones outside. The other kid who I was supposed to fight wasn't as big as me because I was a tall chubby kid for my age. He had a flat-shaped head. "What's up now?" he said.

My hands were sweaty from being nervous. I looked around at the spectator before the other kid could say another word "Pow!"

I punched him dead center in his mouth and followed up with another punch to his forehead. He fell backwards on his ass, holding his mouth. I was wondering if the others were going to jump to his rescue, but instead, they just stood around and looked. One of the other kids tried to help him up. I knew this fight was over. The next morning, Umar and I had our choice of seats. Even the tough-looking brother and sister in our class tried to make conversation. From that day on I learned another lesson. Swing first! Don't be fooled by looks.

Chapter 09

"There are two things over which you have complete dominion and control- your mind and your mouth."

—Yoruba Proverb

I remember my father taking me to the barbershop on 15th and A Street for a haircut. The whole 15th Street, from 15th and Pennsylvania Ave, S.E., to 15th and G Street, N. E. was a drug strip. In many areas like these, the majority of the population were Afro-Americans. The more populated it was with blacks, the more poverty, drugs, violence and liquor stores there were but also, you'll see more churches on the corners in the black neighborhoods. The black community, liquor stores and churches go hand and hand. Pray on Sundays up the street and drink all week down the street.

The barbershop my father took me to was across the street from a Catholic School called "Holy Comfort" but on the corner, guys sold dope, and drank liquor. Inside this shop was mostly occupied by older guys. I was the only child in the shop getting a haircut. These old guys who cut hair and the older guys who were getting their haircut always had some type of debate going on about something. Either it was about politics, racism, women, sports or the economy. These old guys took about 40 minutes to cut one person's head because they were talking more than they were cutting. Once they finished cutting someone's hair, it looked like the client's hairline was either crooked or pushed back. My father liked these types of conversations because he loved to debate too.

My father and I walked home down 15th St., passing all the dope pushers, dope fiends, and alcoholics. You could see guys in the alley shooting heroin in their veins, beside old abandoned cars. Drunks, walking up to my father asking for change to get a drink, it was a regular occurrence during our trip back home from the shop. A few addicts even tried to sell my father cheap jewelry, just to get a fix. This was Washington, D.C., the nation's capital but when others see Washington, D.C., on television, they see the White House, the Capital, the monument or the Lincoln Memorial. Ronald Reagan was our President at the time, and this was his hidden treasure. Poverty, Dope pushing and junkies.

A Fork in the Road

My father told me while almost home, "Son, you see those people back there, hanging on the corners, selling drugs, getting high and drinking their lives away?"

"Yeah Dad," I said, wondering what was next and why he'd asked.

"That's just an example if you don't get a proper education, and don't listen to your parents. Those guys out here selling drugs won't last long. Either they're going to jail or someone was going to kill them. Friends will kill friends over a few extra dollars," my father said.

His hands were in his pockets with a thin blue windbreaker jacket. It was kind of windy outside. The leaves were falling and it was gloomy outside right before it snowed.

I thought to myself, "I never want to live a life like those people back there." We were entering our backyard and my father said, "Son, watch your company because you don't have friends, you only have associates. Friends were rare, never ignore the slightest signs of envy and jealousy because what a person says was what's on their heart. Another thing, stay away from getting high, drugs cloud your thinking and decision-making."

I never forgot what my father told me that day. the true wisdom was, "Did I follow what he told me?" We can receive good knowledge all the time from people of all walks of life but the wisdom comes from real-life experience.

It was these older teens, who stayed across the alley from me, Charlie and Larry. Larry was around 14 years old. He was tough as nails and wild. He was known for doing crash-dummy shit on his bike and repairing our bikes when needed. He moved to N.C. several years later and contracted AIDS. He passed away in 87.

He had a little cousin named Romelo "aka Rome." He was a few years younger than me. A skinny kid with legs that looked like spaghetti noodles with a knot in them for knees. Rome was light-skinned, with a bush that looked like he had mixed blood.

His nose was pointy, like a Caucasian, and his mother was dark-skinned, she was young, about 21 years old with a beautiful figure. She had Indian heritage and her boyfriend was a fat sweaty black guy who drove a van.

When he came over, he always kept his van in the alley. He never went inside Rome's mother's house because Rome and his mother were living with his grandmother. His grandmother was very religious. She had Rome playing drums for the church as a kid.

His grandmother didn't approve of her daughter's boyfriend, so she kept him outside. We used to smell reefer coming out of the van while we played basketball in the alley. Then after 15 minutes of seeing smoke coming from the van, we witnessed the van rocking side to side. My friends and I would walk past the van just to hear Rome's mother making these poodle sounds like this fat Pig was doing some damage. After about 2 minutes, the Van door slides open and his mother gets out switching with the little Charlie Angel shorts.

Then the Van would crank up and pull off. Rome liked following us around but he was too young to tag along. So, he vanished for a few years because his grandmother sent him down south with his father.

My mother mostly drank on weekends or sometimes during the week. She would stop by Albert's liquor store, and buy a fifth of Vodka and orange juice. I didn't like when she was drinking because I knew there was going to be an argument all night between my father and her. My mother became a different person when drinking. She would stay up all night until 3 in the morning playing oldies. I could hear the music playing in the basement. My father was in the bedroom.

So, I tried to go downstairs and get her to put her records up and shut the record player off. My mother would have records disseminated all over the floor. She would have the Four Tops playing on the record player. I hated some of the songs because she would play them to death!

"Ma! Ma!" I would say while shaking her awake, because she would be drunk, sitting at the kitchen table with her head in her lap.

"What is it?" she said with a slur.

I told her "Come on Ma and go to bed. It's late. It's almost 3 o'clock in the morning."

She always said the same thing

"One more album."

That one more song or album always ended up being 4 to 5 more from The Temptations to Sam Cook. She liked Sam Cook's music. About this time, my father woke up. That was what I didn't want to happen. That's why I always tried to hurry her to cut the music short, put the records up, and go to bed because when my father woke up there would always be an argument coming.

My father argued about my mother being up all-night

playing music while everybody was sleeping. We couldn't really hear the music while we were sleeping because she would be in the basement playing her music but my father wanted her in the bed, not drunk in the basement all night, playing music.

I could hear my father coming downstairs in the basement. My father was in his cut-off shorts and little T-shirt, barefoot.

"Drinking that shit, playing that music all night while everybody's trying to sleep" My father barked out, pretending to be looking through the refrigerator.

"Fuck you! You fat motherfucker!" My mother slurred out. "You don't tell me what to do!"

From there, it always turned into an all-night argument until 4' in the morning. My sister Tasha slept through all this noise. When I asked her why she never helped me put our mother to bed before our dad woke up, she always said she didn't want to hear it, so she stayed sleeping.

When everybody finally went to bed, it would be about 4:40 am but what amazed me was that my mother would still be up early to fix breakfast for the family and that's Superwoman! But I would be sleepy and tired in class. I grew up hating alcohol and drug usage because of my family.

I called my brother Bay to see if he wasn't busy for the weekend because I wanted to hang out and get something from the mall. One weekend my brother agreed to get me, and we were supposed to be going to the shoe store, but he wanted to stop past his friend Eli's place first.

My brother was driving a black Mercury Cougar at the time. We stopped past Eli's place in Savannah Terrace. Another poverty-stricken neighborhood. You could hear the music coming from Eli's apartment. It was Stephanie Mill's "What You're Going to Do with My Lovin." Eli was a short brown skin guy with a thick mustache like Cheech from Cheech and Chong.

He must have been taking a nap because he came to the door looking as if he'd just gotten out of bed.

"Aye Jack! What's happening?" my brother asked.

"Ain't nothing dude," Eli responded, while yawning.

His mustache looked like a push broom.

"What's on your mind, bro"

My brother pulled out some white top paper and a small manilla envelope.

"Oh Eli, this is my little brother," my brother said, nonchalantly.

He was more so ready to smoke what was in the manila envelope.

I looked at Eli with a forge smile. "What's up"

I knew they were about to get high, so I started getting mad at my brother because I wanted to go to the shoe store.

In the background, Stacey Lattisaw's "I Found Love on a Two-Way Street" was playing on the radio. My brother told me he'd be back, so I waited in the living room. They both went into the backroom. I sat on this black bar stool, stationed up with two other bar stools he had lined up in front of a bar set.

I was looking at the different liquors Eli had behind his bar then I started looking at the pictures on Eli's mahogany coffee table then the strong scent of PCP started sliding under the closed backroom door. I knew my brother was smoking that stuff again.

I started playing with some cards on the bar table, trying to kill time while they smoked themselves into a world of the spirit gods then out of the corner of my eyes, I thought that I saw something moving on the floor like a thick black belt. I looked over to my left and saw a big snake crawling on the floor. I started to holla my brother's name. My brother and Eli came out of the backroom walking like astronauts, walking on the moon.

Eli walked over to the snake and picked it up in slow motion. It was Eli's pet snake that got out of his tank. My brother was standing near the Television looking at the snake with glassy eyes, high as a kite.

"Man, it's only a snake," my brother said, talking so slow that you could hear every syllable in his words. "Eli, we bout to split Jack. I'll talk with you later."

Eli caressed the snake, putting it back in the tank. "Alright man," responding in a low tone. His mustache hid his top lip.

We left his place, and my brother took me back home. He had forgotten that he was going to take me to the shoe store. I asked him, "Why are you taking me home?"

I thought we were going to the mall. He looked puzzled. He said "Oh yeah, I forgot. I'll take you next weekend" I was so damned heated. He never took me, until the following year before Christmas. The shoes I wanted were out of style by then.

Chapter 10

"When you stand with the blessings of your mother and God, it matters not who stands against you."

—Yoruba Proverb

In my sixth-grade class, we had a few guys and females who had the IQ of a grapefruit, but they made up for being dumb by being the class bullies. These walking pineapples were around the age of 14-15 years old in the sixth grade.

We had a selection of good bare-knuckle fighters in our school and neighborhood. Either they were in the boxing gym or just natural. It was the highlight after school watching a good rumble between two good fighters. They weren't toting guns during those days; disputes were settled with the knuckles.

I remember one evening a fight was scheduled between two hard hitters. A boy named "Black" who was 14 years old in the 6th grade, with a Jet-black complexion. His knuckles were always ashy from either fighting or just plain lack of using lotion. He had a scar over his right eye from constant brawls. He had broad shoulders, and strong legs and walked with his fist constantly balled up. He was sitting older teens on their ass. His record was undefeated.

The other kid was named "Head" he was a 5th grader, around 13 years old. A brown-skinned kid with a funny-shaped head that looked like a sledgehammer. He had a missing tooth from brawling with his mother's boyfriend. The guy had put his hands on his mother and Head punched her boyfriend in the neck while he was putting on his shoes. Her boyfriend smacked Head in the mouth with a pair of size 12 Stacy Adams.

Those hard-ass shoes knocked Head's tooth out. Head was boxing under the number 10 gym. He had long arms and a short torso. Pigeon toed and fast. His record was numerous wins and one loss.

Black and Head, met up in front of a huge green dumpster, near the teacher's parking lot. Black had a toothpick in his mouth. Everybody was standing around waiting for the first blow. Black asked Head if he was trying to see him with his hands.

Head said, "Yeah, it's whatever!"

A Fork in the Road

Black asked his sister to hold his books as if he could actually read. Head laid his books behind the dumpster. They both put their hands up, fist balled tight. Black had hands like a brick. Head was fast with his hands. They both went straight at each other.

Black landed a punch dead center into Head's forehead. You could see a knot growing the size of a golf ball. But Head didn't buckle instead came back with a strong jab, which only landed on Black's shoulder. Black delivered another strong right, dead center into Head's left eye, causing a deep gash. Head was starting to break out into a sweat. Still, he didn't back down. Head threw a lazy left towards Black's right, causing Black to lean slightly over to his left, but Head timed him perfectly, following up with a strong right, catching Black straight in the mouth, and knocking Black's tooth out.

Everybody said "Ohh!" Then Head started throwing punches like his life depended on it. Black shielded his face with his forearms while Head kept delivering blows. Head started getting tired. Black saw his opportunity to come back.

Black grabbed Head's shirt and buried his fist straight into Head's face. Then another hard blow to the forehead. Head was trying to get out of Black's grip. Black landed another punch straight into Head's gash eye, causing the cut to open up more. Head went down on one knee.

Black punched him again, until Head said "Ok, I had enough! You got it!"

Black sister said "Stop! He has had enough" The fight was over. Black won the fight and remained undefeated.

Everybody started walking away, heading home. The next day in class, it was the talk of the school until the teacher said "Be Quiet!"

Me and my Friends sat outside on the brick wall contemplating what we should get into.

Keith said "Let's play some tags"

Chuck looked at Keith with aggravation "Don't nobody want to play tags, you retarded motherfucker"

Touch said "Let's flip quarters" It's a game in which everybody tosses their quarters up against the wall, and see whose coin landed the closest to the wall. Whomever coin lands the closest takes everybody else's.

Me, Keith, Chuck, Charles and Leo started pulling coins out of our pockets. We each started tossing our coins up against the brick wall. Leo was the closest. He had won six tosses in a row. Leo was a natural when it came to gambling because his uncle taught Leo how to shoot dice and cards and play with numbers at an early age.

Driving down our street in a burgundy 82 Ford Thunderbird with a white vinyl top was, "Dedo" and "Taylor." These two older cats were known for stickups and kidnapping. They pulled up in front of us, and called me to the car. I walked over wondering why they called me.

I leaned over on the passenger side window, asking Dedo. "What's up?"

On his lap was a huge 45 automatic, with a brown handle. Dedo wanted to know if I saw a Green Mustang drive down my street. I looked over at Taylor, who was driving. He was a huge jet-black heavy-set guy with large hands. He had his hands gripped around the steering wheel.

In his lap was a sawed-off shotgun. Dedo was a short stocky guy with a thick neck, like a tree trunk.

I said "Naw, I didn't see no green Mustang drive down my street" Dedo looked over at Taylor, then towards me.

"Alright, step the fuck back, let's go Taylor" I stepped back and they haul their ass down the street, and turned on

19th Street. Everybody had stopped tossing coins and started looking at me.

"What did they want?" Chuck asked. I told them they were looking for someone. Everybody stood in silence for 15 seconds, then we went back to tossing coins.

Chapter 11

"When you strengthen your self-esteem there is no room for jealousy."

—Yoruba Proverb

The year was now 1983, we used to ride our bikes through Congressional Cemetery. We would come from the back of the cemetery, coming from the DC General Hospital parking lot near The DC Jail side entrance. The fence had a hole cut out but we had to exit through the front of the Cemetery because the "putt-putt" (Security officers) were riding around in the DC General parking lot.

The Congressional Cemetery was a 35-acre historic burial ground located on Capitol Hill in Washington D.C., on the west bank of the Anacostia River. It was the only American "Cemetery of National Memory" founded before the Civil War. Buried there were Elbridge Gerry, J. Edgar Hoover and Matthew Brady.

We hung out in the cemetery until close to 6 pm, then we

headed out. The cemetery became our meeting spot for years until eventually many of us became a resident amongst the dead.

I started playing on the school basketball team "The Payne School Wildcats." I played the Center position. Our uniforms were dark blue. I hated doing the suicide drills because I was chubby. We had to run as fast as we could halfway and back. By the time we reached halfway through the court, I felt like I was dying but I tried to hang in there since our coach was a hard coach. Our coach was Mr. Crawford, and Mrs. Slone was working with the Cheerleaders.

I remember playing our first game. We had a prep rally, in which everybody in the school was invited to the gym. When we had our scrimmage, with just a few people watching, I was ok but when I saw the crowd for our regular game in the gym, hyped up, and cheering, I got nervous.

It was teachers, staff members, and everybody from every class in that gym, but what really made me nervous and freeze up, was when my mother came walking into the gym and sat in the bleachers, in her work uniform. Man, I wanted to just sit on the bench. But eventually, Mr. Crawford called me into the game to give the other Center some rest. I was nervous and clumsy. I played terribly. I made it up in another game, at the other team's house. I got rebounds and scored 6 points. Our team went to the playoffs but got knocked out of it. I was crushed because I had started getting into the hype but our season was over. I had gotten my first trophy. My father put my little trophy with my brother Frankie's big trophies. My brother Frankie had trophies everywhere.

I even started playing on the basketball team for the boys and girls club, during the summer. We made it to the Championship but lost. I had lost so much weight over the summer, playing basketball, and football, running around with my cousins and friends in the streets. When I started Junior High school, I was a new person. 'Wait until they see me now,' I thought to myself.

Chapter 12

"You can't solve the problem because you don't know what it is."

—Yoruba Proverb

My grandfather was dying of cancer. It was hurtful seeing my grandmother cry and pleading with God not to take my grandfather away from her. My grandfather was all she ever knew. I remember babysitting my grandfather while my mother took my grandmother to the grocery store. I had to use myself as a crutch, walking my grandfather to the bathroom. I was eleven years old at the time. I noticed when a lot of people get close to death, they start to see a glimpse of the other side and want their lives here to hurry up and be over with.

My father had just retired after working 22 years for the Navy Base. So, he did a lot of chores around the house. When I got home my father was cooking dinner. My father was a good cook. My dad made everything from Scratch. He had a lot of free time around the house, to get things done but on this day, my father looked like he had something to say.

A Fork in the Road

"Hey son, how was school?"

"Fine Dad," I said wondering why he asked.

He looked like he was hesitant about what to say next.

"Son, your grandfather just passed away this afternoon. Your mother and everybody's at the hospital."

I was thinking to myself, that I was just over at my grandparent's house for lunch. My grandmother and Uncle didn't seem like anything was wrong, but come to find out my grandfather had just died after I left, while in the hospital. This was a sad day for the family because we just lost the head of this family.

I was out of school for a day, due to the funeral. The next day at school I saw familiar faces of guys and females from my side of East Capitol Street, and new faces from the opposite side of East Capitol. East Capitol Street separated the South-East side from The North-East side. I saw some of the students in my Grandparent's neighborhood on the North-East side. We glanced at each other but kept it moving. While in Art Class, some of the boys from 15th & C St. N.E. wanted to compare their neighborhood with my neighborhood on 15th & C St. S.E. but I let them know that we have knockout artists on our side of town.

That was how I met one of my later best friends because he kept laughing and agreeing with the one talking. His name was "Mandy." Mandy was short with a blockhead, always smiling.

Gary, a fat kid from around Mandy's neighbor laughed at everything Mandy said, in agreement. It was irritating.

When I first met Gary, I thought he was just a sidekick to Mandy, because he just laughed at everything Mandy said. Later going into our 8th grade year Gary became one of my best friends.

Eliot Junior High was a school that resembled a training ground for future street hustlers, Murderers, Stick-up boys and hall-of-fame boxing champs. In the hallway, cutting class were little Boo and Jolie. Two short bullies who were always trying to check the other kid's pockets. Boo always kept a pocket knife on him, and he was willing to use it. Also, at our school were Donald G, Big Clay, Naa new and Cory. Knockout Kings from the North East side of town. On the Southside were Moe, Donae, Joe, Tim and Earl. All Knockout Champs. There were others in the school.

A Fork in the Road

A Lot of the boys at my school and around the neighborhood trained in the evening at Ham's A.C. boxing gym. Boxing was a loved sport in Washington, D.C. and Philly. The kids who didn't know how to fight or didn't have heart got pressed for their lunch money.

I started playing for my school basketball team, the Eliot Lakers.

This was the era when I traded my AJ Jeans in for the Bugle Boy Jeans with the big pockets on the side, Ewing Adidas and Ocean Pacific Shirts. The New Edition was pumping "Cool It Now" and "Mr. Telephone Man" on the video. Grandmaster Flash and Rapper delight jammed on the boombox of every urban neighborhood.

Being from Washington, D.C., Go-Go was the traditional trademark that separated us from any other city or state. A lot of guys in Burgess Gym worked the speed bag off the sound of "Lil Benny and the Masters." The older guys liked the sounds of "Trouble Funk" while drinking brandy on the street corner. Junk Yards, "Sardine and Pork and Beans" was the anthem on the south side of the D.C. Barry Farms project. Rare Essence was the anthem on the Northside but everybody all over the city loved "The Godfather of Soul," Chuck Brown.

Chuck Brown made the guitar talk another language, giving it a smooth mellow sound.

This was our culture! D.C. Culture!

Chapter 13

"All bad habits are not learned in the household, but through who has the most influential effect."

—Yoruba Proverb

The year was 1984. I remember Charlie, Chuck, Dre, Leo, Mel, Chi, Mike B. and I sitting outside in front of the corner store thinking of ways to make money. Driving slowly down the street, gliding past us in a black Cadillac, with white leather seats, was a known heroin dealer named "Birdie."

He was talking on the car phone, wearing a black brim hat, looking like a mad man. Birdie was a short brown-skinned guy who wore wire frame glasses. On his tags read "Birdman" Birdie used to hand the kids money for ice cream when the good humor truck used to roll through. His partner was named "Ryan" who drove a Black Porche. They both were making $15,000 a week, pushing heroin called "Tyson," named after the boxer, in the southeast area.

Chi said, "I want that type of money."

We all wanted that type of money, but I didn't want the problems that came with it, I thought to myself.

One day, my brother Bay and his girlfriend's youngest brother went out to Virginia to meet my cousin and her boyfriend Foster. The Go-Go band Lil Benny and the Masters were playing outside in the park. When we got there, my cousin and Foster were already there. They were looking for the smoke man, so they could cop some more smoke but they already had one joint on hand.

"Let me hit that joint," my brother said

The joint was rolled up on Top paper, stuffed with PCP "Angel Dust." My cousin handed my brother the joint.

"Bay! Me and Foster are about to walk up towards the water fountain and wait for the guy to get here. Save some of that me and Foster because we're trying to smoke too," said my cousin.

Foster had just gotten out of prison. He stayed in and out of the system. He was tall and skinny, wearing a fishnet red shirt, some shorts and sandal-type shoes, with his three-ring socks pulled up to his knees. He was chewing gum, and wearing dark shades. This was the 80's look back then. The park had a lot of people crowded in front of the platform that Lil Benny and his band were playing on. The air was polluted with Marijuana smoke, coming from different smokers but my brother was the only one smoking that "Whack Attack."

The music was jamming, and everybody was grooving to the sounds of the Congos. My brother was puffing the joint real slow, and the fire was burning leisurely, giving it a longer enjoyment. Me and his girlfriend's brother were looking at my brother smoking and dancing at the same time, to the music. He was doing "The snake" dance, moving his upper body side to side like a serpent. It seemed like every time I took my attention off my brother and paid attention to the band then focused back on my brother, his movement became shorter and shorter. The "Love Boat" (PCP) had kicked in. After five more minutes, my brother was a zombie. He still had the joint in his hand, holding it up to his mouth, motionless. But in his mind, he thought he was still moving, because his forehead muscles were still moving, while his eyes were wide as two grapefruits.

When I saw my brother stuck like a statue, holding on to the joint by his mouth, I said to myself, 'this is some Richard

Pryor shit.' Let me go look for my cousin. I found my cousin and led her back to my brother. When my cousin approached my brother, I thought she was going to try helping my brother come down. But instead, she was more concerned that he had smoked the majority of the joint.

"He needs help!" I told her

She said "Damn Bay! You didn't save us none."

I was wondering, 'How are we getting home?' I looked at Foster, who looked like a tall licorice stick, with all these bright clothes on, looking down at me, chewing gum, like a cow chewing grass.

"What's the problem shorty?" he said, in a slow, deep tone.

I looked at him while he was talking, and it seemed like he was talking in slow motion. My cousin took the remaining joint from my brother and then started walking my brother around the park, trying to bring him down. My cousin walked my brother to the car and opened the door, guiding him inside, and placing the car keys in his hands. She even had to guide the keys in the ignition for him, because my brother was on a spaceship, trying to find his way home.

A Fork in the Road

I asked my cousin "How is he going to drive? He's not even on our planet right now. Why can't you drive us home?"

She said she couldn't drive us home because she was waiting for someone. Then my cousin handed him a hot dog from off the grill. She turned the ignition to the car and told my brother to drive safely. His girlfriend's little brother was in the back seat crying because he thought we were stuck in Virginia. I was looking at my cousin, and thought to myself, 'drive safe?' My brother was about to have an accident on the road.

Slowly my brother started driving the car, with me in the front seat, guiding him to the exit of the park, before driving out into traffic. I had to let my brother know when to pull out the exit and turn before the cars came. He was driving so slowly that I could've gotten out and got home quicker on foot. Traffic was beeping their horns because he was holding up traffic. I guided him all the way home just by watching the signs back to D.C. When we finally got to my block, I couldn't wait to get out of the car. We pulled up in the alley in front of my yard. I jumped out and went into the house. My mother was cooking gravy pork chops when I knocked on the back door. She let me in and asked where we went. About this time, my brother had put on his shades and was walking in the backyard. My mother knew when I went straight up the stairs that something had happened.

She looked at my brother with those dark shades and knew he had been smoking again.

"Take those damn shades off, and let me see your eyes," my mother said.

When my brother took off his shades and she saw how red his eyes were, she got mad.

"Didn't I tell you not to smoke that shit while you have my baby with you!" she said, gritting her teeth.

My brother made a phone call and left, taking his girlfriend's brother with him home. My mother stood in the kitchen with her hand on her hips, shaking her head.

I started studying German history and the history of Native Americans. The Apache Indians were my favorite, because they were very skilled fighters, and they were rebellious to the white man the longest. Geronimo, Nina, and Cochise fought to the last man, before surrendering to General Nelson O. Howard. I was a history buff. I was an admirer of great generals, conquers and leaders. I took these attributes with me in the near future.

I met a big-headed kid named Jamaal. Jamaal was a shit starter, always intimidating the off-brand and unpopular kids.

Jamaal always kept a sneaky smirk on his face. Some of the girls in school were scared of him because he would bully them for their phone numbers but a lot of the aggressive females liked him. I never had a problem with Jamaal. I liked big-head Jamaal. He was boxing for Ham AC. like a lot of the young men in the neighborhood.

Also, gangs were forming in my city, like the A-team, The Hill Boys, The Gangster Chronicles, The 8th and H Crew, and the Ghost Busters. These weren't structured gangs like in Los Angeles, and Chicago, but local gangs in the neighborhood. The majority of these gangs fought other neighborhoods and other gangs. You may have one member carrying a 38 revolver or a small .22. The most popular weapons were bats, chains, bricks and a broken bottle. The prosecutors and Judges eventually dissolved the gangs in D.C. after a woman was allegedly sodomized by one of the gangs. They were sentenced to natural life. This was a short life for gangs, but the birth of Drug Crews.

Chapter 14

"No man can serve two masters...or else he will hold to one, and despise the other."

—Yoruba Proverb

I slowly started losing interest in the school programs and academics. I had changed my old associates who were considered not popular and started hanging around a different crowd.

It was me, and my friends. Chi was always doing something mischievous. Sometimes Sye, Andre and Mike would be roaming the streets as well when we used to cut school and hang around other schools. We sometimes saw Jamaal already cutting school, hanging out on the corner. Jamaal had already got into street life early. He was 11 years old when he started hanging in the streets. Some of my friends had already started doing crime and making moves.

I wasn't doing crime at my age. Chi, Chuck, Jamaal and Sye, were coming to school wearing Serac sweatsuits which cost $350 dollars for the whole sweatsuit. Lamont, Moe, Donte, and Mel were wearing Fila and Sergio Tacchini's Sweatsuit, costing every bit of $450 dollars.

Coming up I was leery of street dealers, because I remember as a child, while in the car, my mother would point at all the street peddlers, hustlers, and Con men hanging on 15th Street when we would drive by.

"You don't ever want to get in that life. If you ever get somebody's money wrong, or you lose their product, those types of people will kill you. Work and live an honest life, like me and your father."

So, whenever I encountered those types of people I always went in another direction.

I was going to the barbershop by myself now, on 15th and A street. This whole area was flooded with hustlers, drug users, con men, stick-up artists and gunslingers. On this day I had just gotten my haircut after school. When I was coming out of the shop it was this big-headed light-skinned, older guy on the corner of A Street, right near the barbershop.

"Hey young man!" he said when I passed by him. I was going to keep walking but I stopped when he called me again.

"Hey, young man! Let me holla at ya," he said, wearing a long leather trench, and a leather hat, like Eddie Murphy wore when he did the stand-up comedy "Raw." He had some EK shades, with the snakeskin around the top of the frames, and gold rings on both his pinky fingers with diamonds.

"What's up young man?" he said. "I see you just got a haircut. You fresh shorty! How old are you?"

"Thirteen," I told him.

"You like these shades I'm wearing?"

"Yeah they're ok," I said, wondering in my mind, why he was stopping me.

"Here, you can try these on," he said, handing me the $100 pair of EK shades.

I took the shades but didn't put them on my face. Instead, I just looked at them and handed the shades back to him.

"They're ok," I said

Beep! Beep! Beep!

He swung his coat open and pulled out his beeper.

"Damn, who's this beeping me!" He said, looking as if he had some serious business going on through the number that just appeared on his beeper.

He clamped the beeper back on his belt and pulled out a knot of money.

"Shorty, I know you wish that you could have this type of money," he said, with a nefarious look in his eyes.

"I have to get home," I told him, walking away as fast as possible.

I thought about what my mother said, about these types of guys. He's trying to get me on one of these corners and have me selling his shit. Knowing that as soon as I mess up, he's going to kill me about his money. Eventually, I saw this same guy a year later, under different conditions.

Chapter 15

"Grandma's hands used to issue out a warning, 'Baby don't run so fast,' there might be snakes in that grass."

—Yoruba Proverb

During the summer I signed up for the summer youth program, by Mayor Marion Barry. He made it eligible for our youth to work summer jobs. Everybody had to sign up down 500 and C streets, N.W. My first summer job was as a tutor at Weather less Elementary. My job was to help tutor the 2nd graders. My mother drove me to work each morning and picked me up. I liked tutoring because I like helping people learn. My father always said that a man without an education was an empty shield. Some of the kids wanted me to draw cartoons for them because they saw that I could draw. So, what I would do was tell them that whenever they get a good grade, I'd draw them whatever character they wanted drawn, and I was going to bring some candy to class.

A Fork in the Road

I worked a summer job every summer until they changed the mayors. When Washington, D.C. changed the mayor to Sharon Pratt Dickson, a lot of us couldn't get a summer job any more. She started cutting the number of children who could work depending on one's family income. This opened the doors for a lot of restless teens to get in trouble. I was one of the restless teens, who really wanted to work. The news revealed that this new mayor was misusing the funds.

The times had changed and the people had changed. I even saw a change in me too. My parents were going to send me to Fishburne Military Academy in Pennsylvania at first. My father wanted to see me one day as an officer in the military because he didn't like my company. He felt my friends like Chi, Chuck, Charlie and Leo were trouble. He didn't mind Charlie, but he felt Charlie brought about Chi, Chuck and Leo. He liked Fiche and Keith. Because Fiche helped him a lot in the yard like he was his son too. Keith was quiet and polite. I liked being around Charlie, Chuck and Leo because they were with all the fun stuff.

They liked going on 14th Street NW and messing with the Prostitutes until the pimp eventually came over and asked if we were going to pay, if not stray. Leo had a counterfeit $20 bill that he had gotten from his Uncle Charles. The hooker gave him some head in the alley while we sat around like a couple of stiffs.

Some of my friends started hanging around Potomac Gardens "The Gardens" they called it, a known crime area. Chi used to come back from "The Gardens," and pulled out a stack of money that he'd made that day. Sometimes he used to put a twenty-dollar bill in one of his hands, ball it up and tell me and Charlie if we could guess what hand the money was in. If we guessed correctly we could have the $20 bill. He was playing with money like trash. We were only fourteen and fifteen years old. Just looking at this made me want some too.

But I refused to hustle drugs to make money because I always remembered what my mother said. So, I was always wondering if there was another way.

Chi told us we could make $200 a day just by holding the money after every sale. We would be making $1000 a week. I liked the sound of that, but I wasn't trying to hang in "The Garden" to make money. That spot wasn't safe. I could get killed hanging around there I thought to myself.

"I'll go down there and do it!" Charlie said.

Chi told him tomorrow he could start after school. He asked what I was going to do. I told him I'd pass on the offer.

In my city D.C. Scorpio made it popular to be a hustler after his song "I'm a stone-cold hustler." He talked about the different cars and trucks with rims. The gold chains, and what you do to get these luxuries. Chuck Brown also made it popular living that street life with the song "Run Joe." In D.C. everybody, including my sister Tasha, was wearing the sweatshirt with Mickey Mouse running from the police, wearing a gold rope, beeper, sweatsuit and a bankroll of money falling out of his pocket. Written across the top of the sweatshirt was "Run Joe!" That even became the slang in my city back then. People would greet you with "Wassup Joe!"

The girls became attracted to the drug dealers. They liked the money and fame of these types of people. I remember always seeing Warren drive down our street in his Black Cherokee. I've known him since I was younger. He and his friends were the older teens in our neighborhood. They used to punch our bodies, trying to make us tough. I sat on my porch and Warren always drove by at the same time late in the evening. His truck had big tires, star rims, tinted windows and chrome strip at the bottom of his truck, saying Cherokee. I used to see the light from his truck phone lit up while he was talking. He lived around the corner from me, but he had family on my block. After he parked his truck, he would get out with the whole phone kit in his hand, and go up the steps, into the house.

My mother started taking me to the RFK stadium parking lot, and teaching me how to drive. Since my father stopped driving after the accident he never moved a car again, so he wasn't a good candidate. After studying for my learners, me and my mother went to the DMV and I passed with only one wrong out of 20 questions.

We rode the subway train back home. While on the subway I saw this older teen named "Cucos." He had just gotten out of prison, doing a short bid. He had taken a rap for this big-time drug dealer who paid him $12,000 and brought him a jeep, in which he spent 5 years in Lorton Youth Center. I always remembered when he helped sabotage our clubhouse when I was younger. It was him, his troublemaking younger brother "Jay," and "Big Dee."

But now he was talking like a changed person after doing jail time. I bet he was a changed person after seeing guys get their heads chopped off with homemade shanks, made out of lawnmower blades.

He told me and my mother that he's trying to live a righteous life now. He said being in the streets isn't the way. My mother liked everything he was saying. She looked at me and said, "Pay attention to what he's saying. He's saying some good stuff."

But in my mind, I was saying, I'm not buying it! This piece of shit is pretending. He's just going through the faze a lot of guys coming out of prison go through when their jail time was pure hell. He eventually went back to the streets and later got killed. He was shot in the head 6 times.

I was sitting on my front steps when I saw Warren come driving down our street as he normally does. I waited until he got out of his truck and I called him.

"Hey, Warren!" I shouted up the street.

He stopped in front of his mom's house, wondering what I wanted. I walked up the street to talk to him. He gave me a look of curiosity.

Warren was stocky, 5'9, brown-skinned, low haircut and was heavy-handed when it came to fighting.

"Wassup Warren?" I spoke.

"Wassup? What do you want?" he responded, looking me up and down.

"I'm trying to get some work," I told him

He looked at me with a look of disrespect.

"What type of work??? Because I'm giving you nothing to sell for me, so I can end up getting in trouble for fucking with you. Plus, I don't need you messin' up my money" he said. "How old are you, George???"

"I'm fourteen, going on fifteen" I responded.

He looked at me with a frown, and said "Stay in school and get back up the street"

I walked away feeling embarrassed for approaching him about dealing for him. I started thinking now 'Should I take that holding money job with Chi?'

I laid in my room listening to music. I had a big poster of Salt-N-Pepa on the wall, over top of my bunk bed. Since my sister was now staying in our brother, Frankie's old room. I could now make my little room a bachelor room for myself. The room was small. I could sit on my bunk, and prop my feet up on my dresser but I had it hooked up. Over the top of my dresser was Slick Rick. I had a little star studio radio where I played my Rap music, Doug E. Fresh, RunDMC, Kurtis Blow and Public Enemy #1. I had started courting different females, playing my slow Jams. I thought that I was a player, but two things I lacked. Still no money! Still no Coochie!

I sat on the porch watching Chi, Sye and Chuck ride up and down the street on the scooters they just brought. One had the Elite scooter and the other had the Spree. They were dressed in Moss Brown and Fila sweatsuits, chasing each other. The girls watched from their porches, admiring their outfits and gold chains flying in the wind. The older females asked if they could ride on the back down the street.

Charlie, Touch, Keith and Leo sat on the brick stoop in front of my house. Charlie looked around at everybody and said "We need some money Ya'll!" Leo had already started slinging powder coke. He pulled out a knot of money and said "I'm buying my scooter tomorrow. You all faking!" Leo and Sye were hustling for Rod, on 15th and C St. S.E.

Another older guy who had done a 5-year bid. He was short and light-skinned with a slight Hispanic feature. He talked real slick, always wearing his cap cocked to the side. He drove a blue Audi. His crew wore Madness shirts with his nickname on them "Money Madness." I thought that was some fly shit in my young mind.

Chapter 16

"Lord protect me from my friends; I can take care of my enemies."

—Yoruba Proverb

I was sitting by myself on my front steps when Warren came driving down the street again. I just watched him drive by, but I didn't pay him too much attention because I was discouraged by his last response.

He got out of his truck, with his phone in his hand.

"George!" he shouted up the street. "Come here!"

I got up and walked down the street.

"Wassup?" I spoke

"Come with me" he replied

We walked inside his people's house. His uncle was messing with something in the kitchen. And his mother was watching TV.

"How you doing, Ms. Williams?" I spoke

"I'm ok baby" she replied

"How are you doing sir?" I said to his uncle.

"I'm ok, and yourself George?" he replied

They have known me since I was a kid, playing football in the streets.

"I'm okay, sir" was my response

"George, come down here in the basement," Warren said.

I walked down the stairs in the basement, and he pulled out a safe with some coke in little zip-lock bags.

"Look!" he told me. "I'm going to give you a shot, but don't tell your buddies"

"Okay," I said

"Each bag goes for 25 dollars. I'm going to give you 20 bags to start off with. Give me back 300 dollars," he said

"Come on, let's go outside."

We went outside to his truck. He opened up the back door to his truck and pulled out a wooden stick.

"See this stick?" he said. "If you fuck my money up, I'm going to put this stick on you."

I looked at him in awe, and replied "No, I ain't going to mess your money up."

"Alright, holla at me when you finish," he said.

"Alright," I said, while walking up the street feeling, this was it. I'm now in the game.

I saw Chi coming around the corner. This was during the fall season, and it was getting dark early. It was around 7 p.m. I called Chi and told him I needed to talk with him. He asked me, about what. I told him what I just got from Warren, despite him telling me not to tell my friends, but I thought it would be beneficial to tell Chi because he had a lot of clienteles with the addicts and he knew the ropes on getting rid of this stuff. I don't want to sit on it too long. Chi was more excited about me hustling than I was.

We walked a few blocks to 15th and Independence Ave. SE, looking for customers. It was getting past 8 o'clock. The street looked deserted and it started drizzling. There were only a few stragglers, here and there, coming out of the shadows. This didn't look like the strip I'm used to seeing during the daytime. There normally were junkies, drunks and hustlers out there all day. When it looks deserted all of a sudden, that usually means the police or jump outs (drug task force) have been through, and ran everybody away.

Chi said, "It's been a drought lately out here, that's why I go around "The Gardens" for action. The majority of the fiends have been going down "The Gardens" to cope drugs"

While we were talking, a white lady was walking in the rain crying. She was walking with a black guy who Chi knew.

"Hey baby boy!" the man said. "You have anything, because she's feeling down, and she's looking for a booster."

"I don't have anything on me, but my man right here does" Chi said, referring to me.

"What you have baby?" said the lady.

I showed her a bag, and she peeled out a twenty-dollar bill from her pocket.

"Thank you," she said, and they walked away.

I put the twenty-dollar bill in my pocket, feeling happy that I'd just made my first sale. I didn't stay out there long because it was slow, gloomy and raining, so we left.

Chi kept hugging me, saying now you're in the game. He seemed to be happier than me, about hustling. When I got home, I took my first twenty-dollar bill and hung it on my wall over my dresser, next to my picture of Al Capone, like a legit business. Now I had to hide this stuff from my parents because my parents liked snooping around.

I laid back on my bed thinking, 'I was five dollars short, but I'll make it up tomorrow,' I thought. I got in bed and slept like a baby.

That next day after school, Chi came knocking on our front door. My parents hated when other kids came knocking on our front door, as soon as we'd just gotten in from school.

"Don't these boy's parents make them do homework after school, like we have you doing!" my mother said, while walking up the stairs from the basement, to answer the door.

"Who is it?" she shouted out.

"It's Chi"

My mother looked through the peephole and opened the door. She never really liked Chi since we were younger and she remembered going to his grandmother's house about my pants having berries on the back.

"George is doing his homework. Get with him later," my mother said in a sarcastic way.

"Okay," Chi said, then walking down the steps, wearing a white and blue Hugo Boss sweatsuit.

I was trying to hurry up with my homework, so I could hang out with him. As soon as I finished, I broke out the door. I was trying to catch him before he hit Potomac Gardens. I saw him walking up C Street from a distance. I called him and he stopped. He told me to stick with him. He'll show me the ropes. When we got inside the Gardens, it looked like a flea market.

Potomac Gardens was a project with apartment buildings forming a court. It's located 4.0 miles from the White House. In the middle of this court were some benches, a basketball Court, and a little parking lot for the residents. The majority of the residents living in the Gardena were low-income residents, living off of public assistance, or low-wage jobs. The residents living in this court could barely make ends meet. A lot of the children in this court went to schools nearby, like Payne, Bryant or John Tyler Elementary. A lot of these kids came from single-parent homes with no fathers. No father due to neglect, imprisonment or death.

When I got inside "The Gardens," there were a lot of guys from my old elementary school who weren't fortunate when we were going to the same school. They had to wear the same clothes for days straight with holes in their shoes, and they ate everything you didn't eat from your lunch tray in the cafeteria. But I saw these same classmates inside The Gardens dressed in expensive sweatsuits, Expensive tennis shoes and jewelry, counting knots of money big enough to choke a horse.

Outside Potomac Gardens it looks quiet, like nothing was happening but once you enter The Gardens, it's over 150 people inside this arena, hustling everything. Some selling "Powder," "love boat," "Scramble" or "Water."

They were even selling baby clothes, food stamps, weapons, dinners, and pussy. When I entered this arena, I said to myself, how am I going to get my product sold, with all this competition? I saw one guy with a long line of nearly 30 people waiting to buy his product. He was selling Heroin called "Peter Pan." He told each customer to wait their turn and make sure they had straight money. He told the anxious customers he didn't care if they came with $19.95, they better find 5 cents on the ground. The users put that "Peter Pan" in their hypodermic needle, then shot it in their veins and nodded out to an enchanted world.

Chi walked through The Gardens, introducing me to different guys. One guy he introduced me to was named Looch. I thought he was a fiend when I first met him, because he had big glasses that drooped on his nose and a raspy voice like he smoked all strong generic cigarettes, but he didn't smoke. He had on a jean jacket and jeans that matched. He had on some New Balance boots. But I didn't know he was the reason some of the younger guys were driving a 190E Mercedes, Mitsubishi trucks, Nissan Pathfinder and Maxima.

Chi introduced me to some older guys that were movers and shakers. Some were once addicts turned hustlers who got tired of getting high and started making money. Some people he introduced me to were straight addicts but he was just getting me used to the environment. Some of the teens I already knew from school. Some of the dudes were from the neighborhood. They were shocked to see me down there in such an environment because they knew my past history as a good student who was quiet and did my school work. My parents provided me with everything I ever wanted. So, they were surprised to see me in the trenches just like them, grinding.

Also in The Gardens, it wasn't just guys hustling, but a few females getting money too. One female was named Sal, who had a few workers too. She was light-skinned and dressed like the boys, wearing a sweatsuit, New Balance 995, and walking with a swagger. I leaned up against the apartment wall talking to a few guys then we sat on the bench.

The Gardens have three ways inside this court. So, the police can't come inside without someone hollering "Ola Raids!" meaning the police are coming, because at each entrance was someone looking out for the police. When the police come, it looks like roaches scattering when you cut the lights on. By the time police enter the Gardens, there isn't a soul standing in this court. Everybody was hiding in the apartment building. When the police leave, it's back to a flea market.

One day we were sitting on the bench talking when a guy

came into the court running. Behind him was another guy chasing him with a gun. The guy ran into one of the apartment buildings, losing the pursuer. The guy who ran into the apartment peeped his head out of the building and tried to run around the side of the building but when he bent around the building to get away from the guy, he ended up running straight into him. I could see the shock in the guy's eyes when he ran into the armed pursuer. The guy tried to U-turn around, but the other guy shot him. Then he stood over him and shot him 4 more times with a .22 automatic. I never had seen anything like this in person, only on Television.

I looked at everybody who was sitting on the bench with me and thought they would be shocked too. But instead, they all burst out laughing. I told Glen that the man wasn't moving, he was probably dead. Glen laughed and said, "That's nothing!" Glen was jet black, skinny, a jokester and a stick-up kid. Eventually, he got killed by his own friends while eating some McDonald's French fries. When he got shot in the head, the French fry was still in his mouth when they pushed his body out of the car.

I started with Powder. The hard, which known as "Crack" wasn't widespread in D.C yet, to my knowledge.

A Fork in the Road

When I first saw Crack, Jamaal had some in a capsule. I asked him, "What is that?"

He said "Cocaine, but it's cooked"

I asked "Did it move? Did it make a lot of money?"

He said "Yeah," but I still wasn't convinced.

Before I could pay Warren his money, he had got locked up on a murder beef in Maryland, in which he was an accessory to murder. Warren got out on bond, along with a few others. He eventually beat the case. I paid him his money after everything boiled over. He hit me again with more. By this time, Touch started selling powder for Warren. Everybody I grew up with was doing their thing, including Keith. Keith was a quiet kid who came up with some loving parents. Keith got into the crack market. The only ones who never messed around were Charles, Troy, and Umar. As time prevailed, I realized they made the best choice.

I went to take my driver's test. My father and I caught a cab. I failed the test because I couldn't park in between the two poles. My father waited on the sideline while I went through the test. When I told my dad that I failed, my dad rubbed me on top of the head and said, "You'll get it next time son. Let's get home and get dinner started before your mother and sister get home."

I felt better after that. I took my road test again, but this time it was Warren, and Touch, who came for support. I even used Warren's Truck for my road test. I was used to driving Warren's truck so the test was easier than driving the car from the DMV. I passed the test and finally got my license. I was excited to tell my parents. This was a great day!

I had just been suspended from school because these other boys had jumped another boy in Eliot Junior High School yard, and I wasn't supposed to be on their school grounds, because I was a senior at Eastern High School. Me and Gary were together hanging in the yard talking to a female I liked when all of a sudden these boys started hitting and kicking another boy for his money.

When the principal grabbed the boys for beating the other kid up, we got grabbed too. The principal of the school called our school and told our principal that we were cutting the school on their grounds. My father had to come up to my school to get me back in class. Gary's mother came also. Our principal agreed to let us back in early but I still lost the girl. She left me for another kid who had just bought a Nissan

A Fork in the Road

300ZX. I was heartbroken.

Me and Gary were in the same class at Chamberlain Vocational School. In Chamberlain Career Center, it was multiple trades. We were taking Data Processing. The school bus would pick a lot of us up and drive us back to our high school but we would walk to our High School. Me, Gary, Touch and Bob always stop by KFC for lunch, then head to school. Those were good times.

One late evening, I was chilling outside on my block by myself. Warren pulled up in his partner's Saab.

"Ride with me George," he said.

I got in the car and we went up 1st. Street N.W. looking for his connection. When we got to North Capitol, we turned down Bates Street, going into First Street. Bates Street was a narrow street. First Street crossed Bates. On those streets were row houses. Outside on the left-hand side was a pearl white 928 Porsche. On the right-hand side of 1st and Bates was a white 190E Mercedes. When we turned on 1st. Street, it was guys leaning against the gates and cars. Bend over talking to someone in an Orange Maxima with the kit, who was a tall brown-skinned guy with a bright smile. When we pulled up, it seemed like everybody lifted off the cars and gates to see who was inside the Saab. Warren called out to someone and asked for Tee. The tall brown-skinned guy raised up from the maxima to see who was asking for Tee.

Someone said, "Tee is out of town."

The tall guy with the smile was Rayful. Rayful was supplying 60% of Washington DC with cocaine. His peak net worth was 50 million.

Warren was looking for Rayful's partner, Tee, who had just as much but he wasn't as flashy and flamboyant as Rayful. Rayful rode around the city in a limousine, and turf wars were blamed on Rayful due to his organization. Me and Warren left, heading out to eat at Eddie Leonard carryout, for a Fish Sub. Eddie Leonard had some good food. A lot of the hustlers went to Eddie's after the clubs at night. After me and Warren ate our food, we headed back around the way.

Me and Touch became partners. We both went half on different things. Even meeting females and taking them over to his parent's house, while they were gone to bingo. Touch was getting work from Warren's partner Mac. Mac was getting supplied by Rayful's lieutenant. Everything and everybody were linked to each other in some type of way, and I became a part of it on a lower level.

Chapter 17

"You have to love enough to let go."

—Yoruba Proverb

My high school was a fashion show. I liked coming to school dressed in different outfits every day, but I had to use my brothers to say they brought me the outfits because my parents would get suspicious. In the hallway, you could see certain students wearing Gucci, Hugo Boss, Polo, Tom Taylor, Chanel, Louis Vuitton, Benetton, Moss Brown, Filas and Yves Saint Laurent. After school at 3:00 on the corner of 17th and East Capitol, there was a Carry-out called Gaskin's eatery. This place was across the street from our school. It was always jam-packed. And in front of it, after school, it looked like a car show.

On one side of the street on East Capitol Street Northeast were the girls, standing around wearing big gold earrings, Coach bags, Gucci Links, leather Skirts and fly hairdos, hoping to catch the hustler's attention, so she could be seen in his ride and gold dig for his money.

On the opposite side of the street were the guys standing in front of their cars or on the corner. The majority of these guys were older, in their twenties, trying to catch these teenagers who were groupies for status. Some of these guys were waiting for their runners to get out of school. The difference back then was that the older guys made you go to school, and then hustle later because if the police see a young teen hanging in the streets during school hours, it draws attention. So they preferred you sold their drugs after school.

On the side of 17th Street, you could see a line of cars. Nissan Maxima, Pathfinder, 300ZX, Four Runner, Isuzu Trooper or Toyota Cressida. These cars belonged to the runners who were attending my high school. But the older guys waiting were driving the Benzes, Range Rover and BMW. The guys competed a lot in this way.

One day we saw Looch drive by in the 500SEL Mercedes. Then we saw little Hampton drive by in a 500 SL Mercedes. Then Looch tried to outdo him by buying a Range Rover and a 500 SL. Then a week later, Hampton brought a champagne colored 500 SEL Mercedes and a blue Range Rover. It went on and on since the money was plentiful.

Me and Chi were cutting school together on this day. He

never went to school, because he had a learning disability like a lot of these teens in the streets. He wanted to cut school over this guy named Patch's house. Patch was a light-skinned pretty boy who acted feminine. He was older than us for about 6 years and our senior. He was dealing with Rayful as well. He drove a Red Suzuki Samurai, and a Cherokee with tinted windows. Patch lived across the street from my past Junior high school.

When we knocked on his door, he was just about to leave to go around M Street NE to pay his respects to Gane's family, who had just been killed on Georgia Ave NW. Ganes was around my age. He worked for Rayful as well. Patch didn't want us around him during school hours, but he let us tag along. We all jumped inside the truck and went around M street, but Gane's family hadn't gotten back home yet from the funeral, so Patch went to Maryland Ave NE to check on his workers. Patch pulled up on the crowd of teens and asked the whereabouts of one of his workers. Something went wrong because he flew home speeding and he double parked in the alley. He went into his house and came out with an Uzi on a strap wrapped across the green sweat hood he was wearing. This was the first time I ever saw an Uzi. My heart was racing because I didn't know what was about to happen. He raced back around there and some guys got out of their car and handed him a footlocker bag.

We went back to his house down into the basement. Down in his basement was a baby crib full of money. He opened the foot locker bag and dumped more money into the crib. I never saw that much money in my life piled up like trash. He looked at us and let out a huffing sound.

"I got to count all this money tonight!" he said. "This is all the money I collected from yesterday and today" He continued. "I owe Rayful half of it," he smiled with a look of arrogance. I like the look of all this money, I thought to myself.

I eventually stopped dealing with Warren because I wasn't getting the money I should've been making. He was always running out of work and he was taxing a lot of his workers with high returns on the money. He was more into chasing women and hanging out. So, after the last run, I went elsewhere for my labor, taking risks since I was not benefiting.

I talked to Chi and asked him to hook me up with his supplier. The next day, Chi and I went inside "The Gardens" and he introduced me to his supplier's brother. When I asked to be hooked up, I didn't want to be dealing with his supplier directly, because the guy he was dealing with had very low tolerance. He wanted you posted every day, like a guard in front of Buckingham Palace. He drove around in a white Range Rover with his partner, checking up on his workers, and making sure everything was going smoothly. He sometimes drove his Nissan Blue Pathfinder when he was dropping off supplies.

I started dealing with a new product. No more snow white, but now the hard substance, "Crack."

When Crack hit the market, it brought about destruction and chaos in the black communities. Guys who were once someone lost their swagger smoking crack. Females who we once had a crush on started looking like homeless zombies, from smoking crack. I remember one day a crack smoker said he had a trick that he was about to have sex with and he needed a blast for them both. So I sold him a twenty-piece of crack. He was bragging on her head game, on how good she could suck dick. Me and Charlie said we wanted to see this head hunter he talked about. We walked inside the apartment building, walking up some steps. He opened the door and asked us to wait in the living room. He called us to the bedroom to see the female he was talking about. When we opened the bedroom door, it was a shock to see who this woman was. When I saw her, I said, "No way!!! This is

Darnell's sister!"

She was older than Darnell. Darnell was in my classroom. His sister was gorgeous. We all had a crush on his big sister. Now, she looked terrible. Her hair was in a ponytail, she was in her underwear and bra. Her eyes looked swollen from lack of sleep. She had a white crust around her lips. She looked like she'd been up all night, and she smelled bad. I felt sorry for her. I asked her how she got hooked on this shit. She didn't answer, but just said, "I like it. What's up? You all got some more?"

I said "No, I'm not giving you more. You're Darnell's sister."

Darnell wasn't in the street life. He was a square, doing the right thing. I wanted to show that much respect. Plus, I used to have a crush on his sister. We left the apartment building.

My man Charlie was a freak but even he said "Damn, she looked and smelled bad" We both shook our heads, and walked down the street.

Chapter 18

"To understand how society functions, you must understand the relationship between the rich and poor."

—Yoruba Proverb

Chi bought himself a Mitsubishi Montero Jeep and Chuck bought a 300ZX. I had two shoe boxes full of money in the house. I had just gotten my driver's license, but I couldn't just buy a car like Chuck and Chi. Their household was different. My parents ain't going for it. If my parents ever found out I was hustling, they were going to put me out. I wanted to buy a Maxima with the kit like the guy Duce from L Street. A lot of my friends and people just accepted it and lived off their illegal money.

A lot of the older females started wanting to get with us when they saw that we were making money but a lot of them became washed up over the years. When we wanted them a few years ago, they brushed us off and made us seem like cute pets. Now they were glad if we even drove by and blew the car horn, acknowledging them. A lot of them had gained weight, gotten on drugs or had kids. Nobody wanted these washed-up, early 80's chicks no more. The girls our age were happening. Even the older guys were chasing the new fly girls.

The year was 1987, I ran into my old girlfriend. She had just started going to my school. She saw me in the hallway and hugged me. She said I looked good. I was wearing a Gucci knitted sweater, jeans and a pair of Gucci tennis shoes that I bought from the Gucci shop in Atlantic City, New Jersey. She still looked good, but I wasn't interested in her any more, because now I was on something else. She told me to call her. But I had forgotten her number. Besides, she cut me off for another boy in her class who was driving a 300ZX. He was finished with her, now she wanted to come back to me. I'll pass on this bait, and let someone else have her. She later died in a house fire, which was sad. Her and her family's home caught on fire through a space heater. That was a sad day for us all.

Chi pulled up in his truck when I got out of school. He wanted me to ride with him. We stopped by my house and dropped my school books off. We rode down Potomac Gardens and saw the Range Rover that his supplier drives parked on a side street. Behind it was a yellow Maserati.

When we entered the Gardens, his supplier was standing on the side of the building with two short guys, who were brothers. One was light-skinned and the other was brown-skinned. Chi and I walked over to the guys, and they shook Chi's hand. They all looked at me wondering who I was. Chi introduced them to me.

"Herman, this is George," Chi stated. "He's the one who's been pushing your stuff, through your brother Carlton."

This was my first time seeing this dude. I had heard some stories about him. He was brown-skinned, with a wide nose. He was medium built with a metal rod in his left hand from a shoot-out with the police when he was a teenager, during an armed bank robbery. He did a prison bid, got out and started getting narcotics from the short light skinned guy standing beside him.

"What's up youngin!" he said

He had a slight stutter problem. He shook my hand with a firm grip and asked how old I was.

"I'm 15," I told him

He looked me up and down, and said "Damn, you're a big

youngin!'"

The other guys with him started laughing. Chi introduced me to the other guys standing with Herman.

"This is Sony and Jon Jon," said Chi

Sony owned the Maserati that was parked behind the Range Rover. Sony was Herman's supplier. Sony was about 5'5 with the confidence of a 7-footer. Sony controlled the tempo of the entire Potomac Gardens. He did a prison bid also and started selling barrels full of marijuana for a major connection. He was pulling in $80,000 a week to his connect. But he had a competition that was bringing in $100,000 a week. So Sony killed his competition and became the go-to man.

Jon Jon was quiet but deadly. He owned the burgundy 190E and the Range Rover. Herman just did the driving while Jon Jon sat on the passenger side. He was about 5'6 with a mellow personality.

"Hey, youngin! You need to step it up out here" Herman said. "I'm goin' to flood you with more stuff. You can't be moving like a turtle."

Everybody started laughing again. From that day he started calling me Turtle because I was taking my time, moving the product but I knew it was only reverse psychology for me to stay longer hours on the strip but one thing I can say, Herman nor Warren ever wanted me hustling during school hours. If either one ever caught me not in school, they personally would take me back to school, and make me go inside. They always told me, "You have all day after school to play in mud."

Now I became a part of Herman's clique. He had maybe a total of 12 runners. I started building more clientele than I did when I was messing with Warren. Herman, Sony and Jon Jon liked seeing the young guys get money because it meant more money for them.

One late evening in the Gardens, Sony was celebrating his 23rd birthday. Sony walked through the project wearing a linen outfit and some gators on his feet, holding a glass of champagne. Everybody that night was gambling, shooting craps, hustling, socializing and horse-playing around. Sony walked around observing the atmosphere like a CEO observing his company. Sony had an entourage of soldiers and lieutenants following him around. Guys stopped what they were doing just to say "Happy Birthday Sony!" Herman, Looch, Jon Jon and Carlton, gave Sony stacks of money with rubber bands wrapped around it. One of the young guys from Herman's clique hugged Sony and gave him $200 for his birthday.

"This my man right here!" the young dude said. "I love this dude! He made it happen for us all."

He was intoxicated, talking with his words slurring.

Sony said, "Thanks, I love you too."

The young dude walked to his car later that night. He drove a black 280ZX, parked by the corner store. While he was putting his key in the door, someone came behind him and shot him two times in the head with a .357 revolver. This was a hit from people he trusted.

I liked coming to class and making the girls stare at what I was wearing. It was a few other teens in class who were turning heads too. One of the boys in my U.S. Government class was named Chris, but guys called him "Lil Cee," a fly dresser. Little Cee was getting money, since the age of 14. I liked little Cee. He stuttered when he talked, just like Herman, but worse. Little Cee drove to school in a Mitsubishi Montero, like Chi. Little Cee was 16 years old with his own crew. He later opened up his own strip in Kentucky Courts, on 14th Street

SE and turned a ghost town apartment complex into a million dollar a month Strip, with over 26 workers. Little Cee was killed in 1992 by the police.

I was doing good until one day I messed up some of Herman's money. For some reason, I was coming up short on money and the product. I thought that I was tripping because what I was stashing in another location kept coming up less and less. I gave Herman $2,300, but I owed him some more. When I went to my stash spot to get more to pay him, I didn't have enough. I knew that I hadn't been spending money like that. So I told him that I would pay him extra out of the next supply.

One night in the Gardens I had the money for Herman in my coat that I owed him. Me and a kid named Blob started horse-playing in the middle of the Gardens. I laid my coat on the bench and chased Blob around the building. When I came back, I put my coat back on and walked home. While walking home, I felt my coat pockets were flat. I didn't feel that bulge in my pockets. I dug my hands into my pockets and felt nothing. I walked back inside the Gardens to see if I had dropped it or something. For some reason, the strip was clear. I couldn't find the money.

"Damn!" I said, "What am I going to tell Herman?"

A few days went by, and before I could tell Herman, Chi had already told him. It was around Christmas time because my father was putting up the Christmas lights. The burgundy Mercedes pulled up in front of my parent's house. When I saw the car, I walked off the porch, out of the way of my father's ear reach. Even if they decided to gun me down, I didn't want my father hurt because of me.

Herman got out of the car. It was him, Jon Jon, Chi and Sye.

"Hey Turtle, what's up!" Herman said. "You fucked up my money and didn't tell me."

I didn't have anything to say. I just explained what happened. I was nervous as shit. I know his M.O. but what saved me was the female named Bunny. She came out of the house and stood on her front porch. Herman was a trick for women. When he saw her, his focus immediately went towards her.

"Damn!" he said, "Who's the hell is that?"

Touch came outside on the porch also. Chi called Touch and told him to come here.

A Fork in the Road

"My man here likes your cousin," Chi said.

"Tell her my man wants to meet her"

Chi just wanted to please Herman in any way possible. So Touch called Bunny over to us. Bunny loves materialistic things, so when she saw the Benz, she was all for it. She and Herman exchanged numbers. About this time Herman realized he was there to check on me about owing him money. He told me to be down at the Gardens early in the morning to work the bill off. He told me there wouldn't be a next time, because if this happens again, he doesn't care if my father or whomever was standing there, he won't be coming to talk. I told him I'd be there in the morning with Sye. I wanted to kiss Bunny.

That next day, I was there around 10 o'clock in the morning. He gave me some Love Boat, instead of crack to sell. The Love Boat (PCP) were in large zip lock bags. I hustled the shit out of those sacks of love boat. I made $1,700 within an hour. I hustled out there from 10 am to 10 p.m. I made up Herman's money and I had an extra $3,800 for myself.

Herman and Sony wanted to keep me on the hook, but I told them, I was giving it up for a minute. Herman even tried to tempt me by saying that he would get me some wheels to get around. It was tempting but I declined. I took my money and walked home. I didn't even want a ride home from him. When I arrived home, my parents were on the porch, mad, wondering where the hell I'd been all day. I told them I'd been over at a girl's house all day, watching movies. I was glad that I was out of that.

The next day Sony got killed going to the halfway house. And Herman got locked up a few weeks later on a pistol charge, violating his parole. I later found out the reason I was coming up short on my stash was because Chi was stealing from me. I remember he used to say, stash your stuff under the mailbox with his. He had always been untrustworthy since we were kids.

My brother Frankie came home for the summer. He noticed my change of associates, my movements and how I dressed. He noticed things my parents didn't notice, or at least in my young mind. My brother was sitting on the front porch when I got out of Chuck's car and walked up the steps to the porch.

"Wassup little brother?" he said

"Nothing," I replied while going into the house.

My brother called me back outside. He looked like he had

something on his mind. He wanted me to have a seat on the porch while he went back into the house and brought out a Monopoly game. I was looking at my brother like 'What are you doing? I'm not trying to play Monopoly.' He laid the Monopoly game on our front porch stoop.

He then said, "Come on. Let's have a brother-to-brother Monopoly game."

We started playing, and I rolled the dice, moving around the board. I landed on "going to jail." I had to wait until I got a "get out of jail" card. He rolled the dice and was landing on spots, collecting more money. We played for about 30 minutes and he said, "Let's stop here."

He said, "Count your money."

I counted my play money and only had $200. He counted his money. He had $1,200.

He said, "See where you kept landing? You kept landing on go to jail. Now think about that if it was real life."

I thought about it, but it didn't really register. He asked me, "Are you dealing drugs for Warren?"

"No!" I told him.

121

But in my mind, I was telling the partial truth, because I don't work for Warren any more, nor Herman. But I once did. I could see he knew I was holding back a secret. So I came clean.

"No, but I used to," I said

He looked at me shaking his head.

"Why are you out there messing around with that stuff? Your family will give you anything you want. You don't need to do that stuff!" he said. "Do you think those guys care about you if you ever get them wrong about their money? None of those guys who want you out there slinging their shit, care about you!"

He looked serious. "They're only pretending to be your friends. Believe me! Because I was hustling reefer back in the days, during the early 70s, when you were a baby but I realized all those guys are just looking for were pawns."

I was quiet, thinking about everything he was saying at the moment.

"Now if you got locked up or killed, don't you know what that will do to us all? You're smarter than those guys," He said.

"I see you're going to keep doing it anyway. So at least

122

work for yourself. I don't want you working for nobody. Get your own."

"I need to start from somewhere," I told him. "I have some money, but where do I start?"

My brother looked at me and said some old associates owed him a favor from back in the days. He said that he was going to get me started on my own and said to give him three days.

About 4 days later, he gave me two bottles of water in a vanilla extract container. This was the chemical to wet down the reefer, turning it into PCP. He said you take the money that you already have and buy the reefer but you have to find a supplier.

I ran into my next-door neighbor, Donny. He was originally from uptown, Park Road N.W. He turned me on to this dude named "Doc."

I started buying reefer and more water from Doc, then wetting the reefer down with the water, turning it into "Love Boat." I was bringing this powerful stuff around my neighborhood, bringing about zombies. I was going back to the supplier so fast that he couldn't keep it up. So he turned me onto another PCP supplier named Kev, who lived in the Cavalier building in NW. He was a short guy with a scar on the side of his head. Kev drove a silver BMW. Right after I started messing with Kev, my old supplier Doc got killed. Doc was found dead in his Chevy Blazer.

I wanted my brother Frankie to cut my hair, because Charlie, and his cousin Bill from "The Farms," which was Barry Farms projects in S.E., and I were planning on going to Kings Dominion Amusement Park the next day.

My brother wanted a hit of that PCP in exchange for cutting my hair at short notice. Because the barber shop had closed on me. I gave my brother a sack to smoke. When I sat in the chair for my haircut, my brother plugged up the clippers and just dug into my head like he was looking for a gold nugget. He just kept running the clippers across the same spot on my head. When I looked in the mirror, my haircut like a madman had cut my head. I told my brother to look at my hair.

He said "I'll straighten it"

He did the same thing again and kept digging in the same spot. My brother's eyes were glossy and he looked like he wanted to cry. He was high as a kite. I told him that it was Ok and that I'd straighten my own hair. He wanted another sack to smoke. So I gave him another sack. I went to bed, getting ready for the next day. About 30 minutes later, my mother came into my room and woke me up out of my sleep.

"George! George!" my mother said. "George! Get up! I need you downstairs now!" She said, sounding furious.

I was thinking, what did they find? When I got downstairs in the basement, I saw my father walking my brother around in the backyard, trying to bring him back to earth. My brother had lunch out of his mind. My father had given him milk to bring down his high. Milk was good for bringing down a high. It's something in milk that fights the chemicals in the drug.

"Did you give your brother some shit to smoke!" my mother asked me again. I could see the rage in her eyes.

"No!" I told her

"Who gave you this shit that got you all fucked up like this?" My father asked, "Who gave you this?"

My brother was shaking, looking crazy, with his eyes looking like a deer caught in somebody's headlights.

He looked at me and said, "George, I'm not going to let them know I got it from you."

He said that right in front of my parents. My mother's eyes beamed in on me and said, "Go to your room. I'll talk with you tomorrow!"

I was thinking, damn! He just got me in trouble.

The next day, I got up and went to take another shower because I felt dirty after my brother got me in trouble. Now I had to face my parents. While in the shower, my brother knocked on the bathroom door and stuck his head inside.

"Man, that shit was some good shit!" my brother said.

"I know that I got you in trouble. I'm going to tell them I was just tripping so don't worry" he said.

"I'm not giving you any more!" I told him.

Me, Charlie and Bill were at King Dominion, waiting to get on the "Grizzly" roller Coaster, when Bill looked at my haircut.

"Man, who cut your hair?" Bill said. "It looks like somebody cut your hair with a piece of glass."

It was some girls standing behind us, who started laughing. One was light-skinned and petite and the other one was brown-skinned with glasses. The light-skinned female was from Largo, Maryland. Her friend was from Landover, Maryland. The light-skinned chick offered to ride on the roller coaster with me. We exchanged phone numbers, and later hooked up. I hooked her friend up with my partner Touch. I eventually had sex with her in Touch's room, and he had sex with her friend in his parent's room while they were out for bingo. When we came outside, getting ready to take them home, Mitch pulled up in his BMW. He had just bought it. We all jumped in the BMW and rolled out.

My connection with the PCP eventually faded out. The supplier Kev passed away from Aids, which he contracted from an 18-year-old gold digger. So I got back into the cocaine world, selling Crack. One day I was standing in front of the Carry Out when a frail light-skinned guy approached me asking for a dime rock. The guy looked familiar. I was wrecking my brain wondering where I knew this guy then it dawned on me. That was the guy who approached me when I was younger, leaving the barbershop. He was trying to entice me to work for him, showing off his fancy clothes and money. Now he looked homeless and smelled bad. The crack epidemic had a firm grip on the black community, and I contributed to the destruction.

Chapter 19

"Living with one foot on solid ground while the
other dangles in the cemetery."

—Yoruba Proverb

The music group, Soul II Soul's "Back to Life" thumped out of the White Nissan Pathfinder, driven by some girls from Ledroit Park, North West that Charlie knew. We were now hanging on 15th and Independence Ave. SE.

A lot of guys from our part of town left Potomac Gardens and started hanging on 15th Street Southeast. I could have started hanging on 18th and D. Street NE, because I knew a lot of the guys and we went to school together, but my family lived up the street and that wouldn't have been a good look. So, I chose the best places away from home.

A Fork in the Road

Chi started hustling around 58th Street Northeast, with his cousin, for another supplier, since Herman was now in prison, serving a 7-year sentence.

Charlie leaned against the Pathfinder, talking to the girls, while the rest of us gathered around Chuck's new Acura. Chuck had traded in his 300ZX for the Acura. Twenty minutes later, Rio pulled up in a Red Corvette T-Top behind Chuck's car. Big Rio had on a polo vest, and a Jamaican Rasta hat tilted to the side. Big Rio always kept that joker smile since we'd been in kindergarten together.

The old crew from back in the day was out of the way for the new hustlers. A lot of them were either locked up, dead or strung out on drugs. I remember riding in the car with my mother looking at all the traffic of junkies, hustlers, and gunslingers hanging on this strip, thinking to myself, I would never live my life like that. Now, here I was, living the life I said that I would never live.

The year was April 1989. I had just arrived back on our block, after shopping. Warren was outside washing his truck when he saw me on the way to the house.

"Did you hear what happened today?" he said

"No, what happened?" I replied

"The feds just busted Rayful and a lot of his crew. They even locked up his family," Warren said, "It's all over the news."

When I got in the house, my mother was watching the news. My mother said, they just arrested some big-time drug boy in our city. About 15 minutes later, the news announced the arrest of Rayful Edmond and his organization again on Television. The news reported that this was the biggest kingpin arrested in Washington, D.C. history. The news showed Rayful and his entourage, handcuffed, going into the federal building.

When Rayful got locked up, a lot of guys fell into financial slumps.

One thing the government didn't realize or maybe it was their plan, that when you take food from wild dogs, in an attempt to starve the pack. The wild dogs now start to eat each other. But not only each other, they will start to attack the innocent for food. And that's what happened in the city. The murder rate shot sky-high. Everybody started trying to make money by any means necessary. All these different names started ringing in the city for their reputation of extorting, robbing, kidnapping and murdering. Washington D.C. became an unsafe place to walk.

Warren and I had fallen out with each other over something that was actually my fault, but I also fell out with my partner Touch as well. This life was separating friendships. What kicked off the first blow, was when Warren and Touch jumped Charlie in the recreation Center. Then the return was when Touch House got shot up. It went back and forth. Warren and his crew had the advantage because they were older and had other homes far out, except Touch. We were younger, still living with our parents locally. A lot of the older hustlers and bank robbers liked me, so they funded us with weapons.

One night I had just left a female's house and was walking home.

Another friend who was with me said, "Let's walk through 16th Street as a shortcut."

My intuition told me not to go down that street. I shouldn't be out here late like this, I thought to myself. For some reason, the street lights were out, and there wasn't a car in sight. I heard the sound of a jeep driving up. When I turned around and looked, the jeep was on the curb, and the gunmen jumped out. He had a clean shot at my head, but the gun jammed.

The other guy in the jeep said "You don't let him get away!" I took off like a jackrabbit, being stalked by coyotes.

The guy jumped back in the jeep and started driving behind me, but I ran up a one-way street. I looked over my shoulder and saw the guy's arm aiming the submachine gun outside the jeep. I ducked off in the carryout, not knowing what direction to run.

Then I heard the guy on the passenger side of the jeep say, "No, don't kill him in there!"

So, they drove off. My heart was pounding, and my adrenalin was pumping. I was furious. The guy with me had disappeared. I thought to myself, this was a set-up.

I wanted to get back. I was thinking about what my brother Frankie said when we played the Monopoly game. These guys were trying to kill me. But what really surprised me was when I found out my own relative, who I had introduced in the circle of my associates, had sold me out. He jumped on the other guy's team just to save his own neck and he lied that I had something to do with Touch home getting shot up. He was the orchestrator of the plan. We went through this dispute for 2 years, on and off. A lot of us who were friends coming up as kids started splitting up and taking sides. About this time a new younger group started hanging around us. Warren later said we should talk about it, and we all stopped the beef.

The year was January, 1990. The mayor, Marion Barry of Washington, D.C. had just been arrested and charged with drug possession and the use of Crack in the Vista International Hotel in downtown Washington D.C. He had been a trailblazer in the development of Washington, D.C.

The city had become the murder capital, in which the murder rate was ranking between 450-500 a year. Washington, D.C. had been known as Chocolate City. Washington, D.C. became a majority-black city in the late 1950s after a white exodus to the suburbs.

In 1970, the black population was 71.1% of the city's population while white people made up 27.7%. The police force was mostly populated with black officers. These officers were coming into the black community, shaking down the dealers for money or information. Some were on the payroll of certain known criminals.

I received a phone call from Gary that two young cops were coming through their strip demanding a stay-out-of-jail fee. One of the officers was the brother of a female friend of mine.

He said that I needed to talk to the broad and get her to talk to her brother about laying off and shaking them down. If not, we need to convince her the hard way. I knew what that meant. Either she convinces her brother, or she will end up in someone's trunk. I said that I would talk to her. She's a nice girl, I would hate to see anything happening to her.

The year was 1991. Me, Charlie, Dre, Mike and Erwin started connecting with an older guy named Sam, who ran numbers and set up heists. He once worked for the metro, but left due to health reasons. He had bad arthritis that hindered his ability to stay on his feet for a long period of time. He had a number racker like the lottery, but the difference was the return would be at odds. Poor folks crave quick money for less work. He was good at scheming a good money heist. One heist was robbing the subway. The guards usually wait for the Station manager to empty the money from the machine and transfer it to the subway train, which was the money train. There were no passengers, only containers full of money from each subway stop. The train was guarded by officers who were armed with shotguns. So the idea was to jack the Station manager and a single guy before arriving at the train. So we plotted to hit the subway. Sam knew the day and time. He still had an inside source. There was an elevator and escalator. The elevator would let us out a few feet from the farecard machine, which was the machine would be unloaded by the manager, into a metal container that looked like a steel box on wheels.

The guards carried a revolver during those times. We were supposed to jam them up before reaching the train. Me, Charlie, Dre, and Erwin sat around outside waiting for Sam to hit us on the pagers. Dre felt Sam was bullshitting about the heist.

Suddenly, Me and Erwin's pagers went off, it was Sam. I ran inside the house to call him back.

Sam's voice sounded hoarse. "Catch a ride at the Armory Station in 10 mins."

This was on a Thursday, no rush hour of people. I came outside to let the others know. Dre, Erwin and I ran inside the house. Charlie stayed outside. We had three jumpsuits from the surplus store.

We took off our tennis shoes and put on the cheap black boots we purchased from Payless. We grabbed some pillowcases from inside the linen closet. I had some Halloween masks from my childhood in a bag. We all left out the door. Dre had a sky-blue Honda. Charlie didn't go, he stayed back. We headed to the station. My heart was pounding like some cargo drums. My mouth became dry. All types of thoughts ran through my head, like, 'What if! What if we got caught? What if we get killed? What if we end up killing someone?' By that time we were there. Dre and Erwin jumped out of the car, anxious to get the job done.

We each were armed. I had a black .45 automatic. Erwin and Dre both had Tec. 9's. They both took the elevator down into the station because it would alarm the guard and station manager if they approached from the escalator. Dre had a Sylvester the Cat mask, and Erwin had worn the Howdy Doody mask. I stayed at the top of the escalator as I looked out. I waited for 3 mins, but it felt like 20 mins, before seeing Dre and Erwin running up the escalator with four pillowcases swinging back and forth. We ran to the car and drove off. A few people were watching, but no good samaritans.

Sam was a cautious guy, so he never talked on the phone, instead, he put the street number in the pager. We met on the streets, but the money was stashed over a female's place that

Erwin was screwing. Sam gave us instructions on where to meet with the money. We met up with Sam again 2 days later, and we split the money. I felt like I was truly a part of this life. It gave me a sense of belonging to something more exciting, than just a regular job.

I had been working for the Safeway grocery store, since 1989, inside the Watergate hotel, on the bottom floor. I worked from 5-10 pm as a courtesy clerk, basically a bag boy. Then I was promoted to a variety clerk. Charlie worked there too. He hated it, but our family wanted us to get jobs after school. We still did crime even with a 9-5.

Two days after the subway heist, some guys around the corner from us robbed an armored truck. There were three guys on the heist. They came off like fat cats, but the federal agents hit one of the guy's house, two days later. They had bought new cars which wasn't a smart idea. One of the guys had made a bond. He got shot in the head while sitting in his brand-new White BMW. One of the bullets knocked his left eye into the passenger's side seat. They never knew who did it.

I had dropped out of the 12th grade and started working in the grocery store full-time. I eventually left there after 3 years. Charlie started living uptown northwest, off 14th St.

N.W., because his grandparents caught a whiff that he was dealing in narcotics, and they put him out. I love it in the Northwest area. I came to hang out with him every chance I could.

My nephews started staying over the house with us. My nephews were like little brothers to me, then nephews. A lot of the younger generation that I remember as kids in the alley catching bumble bees in a bottle, selling baseball cards on the block, and asking for a dollar so that they could buy popsicles, were now in their teens. The young teen girls were imitating the generation of girls before them, by trying to finest the other little boys out of their money. Just like the teen boys were trying to imitate the generation of street hustlers before them, by toting guns and slinging drugs.

One young kid I'd known since he was a knobbly little boy, hanging at my fence asking to see my Spider-man action figure was Romelo, whom we called Rom. He was a church boy, turned criminal. Rom started stealing cars, and later selling Crack. I liked Lil Rom. I looked at Rom like one of my nephews. Rom was a smooth youngin, but he was into all activities that generated money. Rom was still skinny, but he kept a big .357 magnum in his waist. He had a lot of good-looking young girls, coming around the neighborhood, looking for him. Some of the girls were older, around my age. But what I didn't like about Rom was he used to beat on some of the girls. He would get mad at them for things like coming past his grandmother's house without calling, or wearing certain clothing his grandmother didn't approve of because his grandmother was a religious nut.

In one incident he slapped the girl because his grandmother said the girl's dress was too short. In another incident, he tried to run the girl's head through the security bars because she asked him to buy her some snakeskin thigh boots. He felt she was trying to play him like a sucker by asking without making a first offering. It was time I had to tell him to stop hitting on these females. Some of these crazy chicks fell even more in love with him. Rom was a loose cannon, but he was team me.

Rom started hanging around some twins from around my Grandmother's neighborhood on 18th and D St. N.E. The twins were two young wild pit bulls. They had a lot of heart for their sizes. Their rivals were other twins from Kentucky Court S.E. The difference between the two was that the D Street twins were cowboys, while the Kentucky Court twins were making money.

Every neighborhood in the four quadrants of Washington, DC was making money, and trying to become ghetto celebrities.

Chapter 20

"God isn't alarmed when we hit rock bottom.
He made the rock."

—Yoruba Proverb

Big Gary came over while my friend China and I were playing "hoops" on the Nintendo game. Gary was living well. He came up in a loving two-parent home like me but he wanted some extra funds as well. Gary collected the money from the workers. Gary came into the room and sat on the little couch in my room. China was sitting on my bed while I sat Indian-style on the floor. I handed Gary some money. Gary had a big cigar in his mouth, counting money, like he was Jake "Greasy Thumb" Guzik, of the Al Capone mob. Gary was so good with money that you could hand him a stack of money and he could tell you the estimate from the size and weight.

Gary liked going to the strip clubs and wasting a lot of money on the strippers. I wasn't into a lot of strip clubs, but sometimes he would drag me with him. Whenever we were out together, Gary always liked to treat us. He would tell everybody, to keep their money in their pocket, He'll take care of the bill. Gary was around 350lbs, with fat cheeks that made his eyes look chinky when he laughed. Gary drove a black Chevy Blazer.

Charlie and I were going into "The National's Jewelry" store in George Town when these two females were coming out of the store. We recognized one of the females from our old Summer job. Plus, she used to talk to our homeboy Chi.

"Excuse me, didn't you once work a summer job in Eastern?" Charlie asked the girl. "Plus, you used to talk to our man, Chi?"

"Yeah," she said. "I do recognize you all now. How are you all?" replied the girl.

She was so thick in the hips, and ass. Her skin-tight beige jeans were so tight that you could count the money in her pocket, without pulling it out. The other girl with her, had on some skin-tight blue jeans. Her ass and thighs were so thick. While standing her legs dropped back as if she were double-jointed, and her round ass demanded attention. She was a paper bag tan, wearing her hair in braids. She had a gorgeous face, with curious eyes, like she wanted to know more about these guys her friend knew from the Summer job.

A Fork in the Road

I asked the girl her name. She said her name was "Rihanna." I laid my spill down and she gave me her phone number. The girls went their way and we went ours. Later that same day, I met another girl. This girl was a Chocolate complexion with curves out of this world. She had a beautiful dark chocolate complexion, with full lips. She said that she was from Trinidad, but she and her friend were visiting some friends who were locked up in DC jail. I wrote her number down on my jeans because I didn't have any paper. And I gave her my number. She said her name was Diamond.

When I got in the house, I smelled of Fried Chicken, collard Greens, Macaroni and Cheese with cornbread. I took a shower first, then ate with my family. We all ate together the majority of the time now that we had one of my nephews added to the dinner table.

I called the girl, Rihanna. She was from Barry Farms Projects, in the Southeast region of Washington DC. I asked her, "You're from the hood?" She got offended and said, "That isn't the hood."

Anybody from Washington, DC knows that the "Farms" they call it, was a rough neighborhood. A Reconstruction Era community for freed people in the D.C. area, which transformed into a site for segregated public housing in the 20th century. Barry Farms got remodeled, but it's still known for crime during the 90's. Barry Farms was a popular part of Washington, D.C. The band "Junkyard" always put their stomping ground, Barry Farms, on display. Barry Farms was also a National Landmark in the city.

Rihanna and I went to the movies together, and out to eat. She was tall for a female, standing about 5'9 with a figure like a video Vixen. She started coming around the house sometimes during her lunch break from school. She happened to be a student attending Eastern Senior High. I didn't know she was two years younger than me. I thought she was 19 years old like me. She looked older than she was. She always asked me what I did for a living. I told her that I provided a service to the women. She smiled and said that I was silly.

Warren and his partner Mitch gave up the drug business and started working as EMTs. Warren had been saying for a while, back when I was working for him, that he was going to take the EMT training. His partner Mitch passed the test first. Warren moved to Virginia, and Mitch moved out of Baltimore, Maryland. They got out of the life while they were ahead. Which was smart.

A Fork in the Road

Mike B also moved out of the city at the right time, with his brother Fred. Mike B had got on Crack while living in D.C., but later cleaned himself up and moved to Rhode Island.

In these streets, you could be ruthless or crafty. Very few knew how to be both because a lot of the guys get caught up in one characteristic and neglect the other. Most guys in D.C. feel the ruthless approach was the way because applying the characteristic of being crafty and the fox, takes patience, which a lot of the guys can't get past their personal emotions. I stayed alive by being crafty. Murder wasn't my thing. Robbery wasn't my thing either. I felt robbing the next person who was trying to eat or make a living just like everybody else wasn't morally right, even though I'd been on a few capers as an extra hand. I love money too, but I prefer to make it off other people's demand. I didn't like the drug business, because it destroyed families. I contributed to the destruction. I wasn't into pimping because I love and respect women. But I still was just as much the problem, as the murderers, extortionists, robbers, and drug dealers, because these were all my friends, for the moment I thought.

I was on the block when Sam and Mik pulled up in a pearl white 92' four-door Acura. Sam was driving while Mik talked on the car phone. Mik had just bought this Acura. Mik had turned Muslim. He went to Egypt and brought back a beautiful wife from the Middle East. Mik stayed next door to Chi. "George! Let me talk to you, Joe!" Sam said while getting out of the Acura. Mik gave me a wave but kept talking on the phone.

"What's up Homie!" I replied.

Sam had a serious look on his face, about what he was going to say. First, he looked over my shoulder to see if anybody was coming in close ear distance.

"You know I believe it's a snitch in our circle nearby, because a lot of guy's places have been getting raided out of the clear blue, in random orders. Do you still talk to that tall redbone who has a brother in the department?" Sam said, while still looking around like we were being watched.

"I'll holla at her," I told him.

One night Diamond was over at my parent's house. Me and her ate carry out while watching TV in my room.

"Bam! Bam! Bam!" was the sound of a loud knock on my room door. I unlocked the room door and it was my mother.

"What is it Ma!" I asked.

A Fork in the Road

"Look outside! It's police officers all over Madison's house. Look outside!"

I walked to the front door and went outside on the front porch. It looked like the whole DEA department was on our block. The DEA had run up in Touch's house, and arrested him, his father and his cousin. The DEA was coming out of their house with scales, pistols and other paraphernalia's.

"See what I mean!" said my mother, "The Madison have been working hard for years to keep a roof over their heads, just to have some shit like this happen." My mother's eyes narrowed in on me. "This is what drug dealing does to hard-working people. The fool who sells it ain't thinking about the risk it puts their family in, by getting their home confiscated. You bet not have that shit going on in our house," said my mother, serious about her statement.

I called Sam and told him I was waiting for my source to get back to me. Sam said, "He got the word already who he thinks is the rat."

"Who?" I asked.

"Erwin," he said.

Erwin, I couldn't believe it. I asked if he was sure. He got

147

quiet, maybe to collect his thoughts. The Feds had Erwin under investigation, and everybody who came around, or in contact with Erwin became a target for the Feds. Four different houses got raided behind Erwin being on their radar. Erwin did the subway heist and other big crimes. His name came across the FBI's desk.

Touch, his father and cousin, later beat the serious charges because the agents didn't have probable cause to raid the Madison's house. But Touch, his father and his Cousin pleaded guilty to the minor charges, and they got lenient sentences.

They were sentenced to 10 years and shipped out to serve their time.

It was the day before Valentine's Day. I caught the greyhound out of Richmond, Va. to spend it with a female friend of mine. When I got back, I got a beep from Charlie. I called him back. He wanted to know where I'd been for the past 3 days because everybody was on edge. I told him that I'd gone out to Richmond to see someone. He wanted to know who she was and if he had ever met her before. I told him no. He said, come outside. I came outside and waited for him. He said, get in the car, he wanted to talk to me.

"You know they found Erwin in the apartment hallway

dead," he said.

"He was shot in the back of the head five times with a .38 handgun."

"Damn!" I spoke. "These guys out here don't waste time when their name gets dirt on it."

I went to visit my brother, Bay, at his apartment. My brother had gotten an apartment across from my old high school. These apartments were low-income apartments. I knocked on his door to see if he was home. He didn't have a phone in his place, so I had to take a chance to catch him home. After two knocks, my brother opened the door. He was glad to see me.

"Hey Lil brother, come inside" he said.

Inside my brother's apartment was a dump. It had dirty clothes on the room floor. He had old beer cans and soda cans with cigarette ashes on top of the can. There were cigarette butts all over the coffee table. My brother looked different every time I saw him. He didn't look like he used to. I remembered seeing my brother as one of the flyest guys in the world. Now drugs had torn him apart. My brother started off smoking reefer, to PCP, now graduating to crack and heroin.

I looked at my brother sitting in the chair, looking frail and broken down. It made me want to cry, seeing my champion torn down like this. He tried to show strength, but I could see it was an act.

"So what brought you to this part of town, dude?" he asked, he looked like he'd been up all night.

"I just wanted to check up on you," I said. "So what's up with you? I got me a new girlfriend named Diamond"

My brother would drift off in a nod, in between statements, then come back to our conversation.

"So, you have a new girlfriend?" he replied.

"Yep" I replied.

"So, what about the other girl?" he asked, going back into a nod.

"Me and her are cool, but we've broken up," I told him.

"Damn, little brother! She was a good girl," he said.

I went into my pocket and gave him $40. He looked up and gave me a sad smile like he didn't want me to leave.

"Thanks, little brother," he said, putting the money in his pocket.

I left the apartment wishing I could get my brother some help.

Lil Rom, Tim and Chuck, were plotting to kidnap Fat Sweat. Fat Sweat was a big fat nasty, greasy hog, who drove a Landcruiser, and he was stingy. His girlfriend was a gorgeous young girl around our age, but Fat Sweat was about 10 years her senior.

Everybody knew she only wanted him for the money. Tim hated seeing a fat grease ball, bounce up and down on something so fine. They  kidnapped Fat Sweat and held him for 13 days until his girlfriend delivered the money at the designated spot. They had him call his girlfriend, and give her the instructions on what to do. When Fat Sweat was finally found, he was on the side of the highway in the trunk of an old Ford Granada, dead with no clothes.

I went over to Chuck's apartment and Tim was over at his place. It was a 9mm and a Glock .40 lying on the kitchen table. They said Lil Rom got his share and left about 45 minutes ago. I had stopped by because I liked to know these guys' mind frames by playing them close for a moment, then disappearing for a while. Because when you're dealing with wolves, you've got to keep yourself from becoming their next meal.

I made small talk, reminiscing about when we were kids, and I left. I saw Lil Rom that night, and he was talking to some girl, double parked in front of his grandmother's house. When he saw me coming, he knew what I was going to say. The girl pulled off when she saw I wanted to speak with Rom.

"I know! I know!" he said, "but the dude was some shit anyway."

I gave Rom my new beeper number and told him to be careful.

One day I was talking to Rihanna when she said that she was going to call me back because her sister had to use the phone. When she called me back, said that her sister had some business to take care of. I joked with her, asking what type of business she was talking about. She said that her sister sold guns. I asked her what kind of guns her sister sold. She told me she sold any kind of guns you wanted. I told her to put her sister on the phone. She put her sister on the line. I asked her sister if she could get me any firepower. She told me that she could.

Her sister told me to get a gun magazine, with all the guns they manufacture in the gun stores, and just give her the name of what kind I wanted. She put Rihanna back on the phone. I told her that I knew hundreds of guys who needed weapons. These guys will pay top dollars for brand-new weapons. She said, just get the magazine, and let her know.

It was 8:51 am. I got a call from Charlie, which was usual at that early in the morning, coming from him. His voice sounded like he'd been crying.

"Wassup?" I asked, still half asleep.

"They found Chi and his cousin Antonio duct taped under Susan's bridge, both shot in the head three times a piece." He replied, with a pause in his words.

Damn, I thought to myself. How did he get cornered like that?

That week, we all went to Chi and Antonio's wake and funeral. Me, Rome, Charlie, Gary, Chuck, Tim, Keith and my nephew sat on the balcony of the church. We all paid our respects to Chi's grandmother. It started drizzling, like most times when someone transitions to the other side.

Afterwards, we all sat on my front steps and talked about old times as kids. Three weeks after Chi's death, Tim and Chuck were found dead in Chuck's Acura. Both had been shot twice in the back of the head. The way they were killed, it came from someone, or some people, they trusted, because they let the shooters sit behind them.

After this, I started spending more time around Diamond. Me and Diamond went to the movies and everywhere together. I met her family, and I liked their hospitality. I started growing tired of this life, and being around Diamond helped me escape being in it.

My nephew started hanging on 15th Street with the fellas. I didn't want my nephew in the life, but he chose to be a part of the life. My nephew didn't do a lot of talking, more so was a good listener. He and Lil Rom started hanging together until later parting ways. My nephew felt Rom couldn't think past his pistol.

I started selling guns through Rihanna and her sister. They were providing me with all types of weapons wholesale and I was selling them at retail prices to the hustlers. Some of my other homeboys ventured off into the chop shop business, stealing and selling luxury cars for half price, with a changed serial number but my homeboy Gary said they'd been taking losses, because of the dirty cops that were taxing them in the area. Some of these dirty cops went to high school with me, but they were the outcast students. Only the head police of these shakedowns wasn't an outcast. He was a basketball star at our school. The females was in love with him. He was tall and fairly handsome. Now he chose the life of a cop who extorts his own people. Two of the cops were females. Six months later these same officers got convicted on drugs and racketeering charges. The head officer and ring leader were sentenced to 15 years in the federal system.

Rihanna came past my house in a brown Monte Carlo, with another guy, her cousin and so-called bodyguard. She said that she was going to pull around in the alley. She got out of the car, and opened the trunk, while the guy sat behind the wheel. I looked inside the trunk and saw all types of weapons. An AK-47, HK, AR-15, a few handguns and a Steyr AUG, which was an Austrian bullpup assault rifle. I never had seen an assault rifle like this AUG. She marketed these weapons like an experienced salesman. I bought an AP-9, .357,.45, 10mm and the 9MM. All for only $750. I sold everything for $1,300.00. I didn't want to get all that big stuff right there on my block, because the neighbors were nosy but I came back and purchased a MAC 11, TECH 9, and a few more .357s. She had a long silencer that fitted the MAC 11.

I was selling so many weapons that the money was becoming more appealing than the narco business but Rihanna eventually crossed me on the guns. She sold me some replicas, and the buyers thought it was a bad joke on my part then she disappeared.

I wanted to change my life. I was in love with Diamond, so why not leave that bullshit behind me. Every time I came back home after being gone away with Diamond, I got more news of another childhood friend killed. Leo got gunned down in the carryout where we all hung out. Rio got shot in the back, paralyzing him from the waist down. Keith got shot up in his BMW while waiting at the red light with his girlfriend. She died instantly, but he lingered for a few days before dying himself in DC General Hospital. Charlie and Black were walking down the street when some gunmen drove by, firing a HK G3 (Heckler & Koch) and pump shotgun, knocking an innocent bystander through the barbershop window. Charlie said what saved him was when he tripped up on a broken sidewalk while running. The HK bullets tore chunks out of the tree bark.

A Fork in the Road

Black rolled up under someone's truck.

But what also disturbed me was when my nephew got robbed late one night on the same street we all hung out, by some snake associate I'd told him to look out for a year ago. A few of the guys were upset with me because they felt I should've been out there near my nephew, instead of always being around Diamond.

So, I called it quits and gave it up altogether. I'm done!

Me and my childhood best friend.

Chapter 21

"You've been tricked! You been had!

Hoodwinked! Bamboozled!"

—Yoruba Proverb

Me and Diamond started living together. I looked through the newspapers and word of mouth on what jobs were hiring. It was rough trying to find a job. I had dropped out of school. That made the search even worse. I was broke and my appearance fell. Sometimes Lil Rom would stop by and hand me money, even helping me with groceries. Rom didn't like seeing me looking this way. My hair needed to be cut. My beard had grown all over my face and I snacked every 15 mins out of stress, causing me to gain 30 lbs. but I was glad to be out of the street life. I eventually had a son.

I like playing with my son at home. He kept me grounded

and occupied with chores. I would visit my parents in the old neighborhood, but I wouldn't stay a long time. Sometimes I may sit out on the front porch and talk to Charlie, Rom and Gary when I decide to stop by but after an hour or two, I was ready to go back out where I lived, nice and quiet.

Me and Diamond were in Red Lobsters for dinner when my pager went off. I still had my pager because I had a few more weeks before it was going to get cut off. The number was Charlie's with 911 behind it. I excused myself from the table and called Charlie back. He said that he heard the police were all at my parent's house. He said I should find out what was going on. I hung up the phone and called my parents. My sister answered. She said my nephew just stabbed some other boy to death in broad daylight, and the police were looking for him.

The police caught my nephew over at his mother's house. The person my nephew stabbed was the one who had robbed him a year ago. The young teen made a dying declaration before passing away in the hospital.

My nephew was sent to D.C. Jail in the juvenile section because he was only 16 years old. Once he got in DC jail he automatically was a new candidate for the Northside and Southside wars. When he first got there he didn't know he had to claim a side or become open season for both sides. So he went with the Northeast side.

I went to visit my nephew in DC jail, and he was brought out in shackles and placed in a small cage, behind the glass, wearing a blue jumpsuit. My nephew had a bland look on his face. We had to talk over an attached phone, on both sides of the plexiglass.

He picked the phone up and said, "You gotta get me out of here. If you can get me out of here, I'm never going to forget it."

When I left the jail that day, I felt responsible for what happened to my nephew. All that night I paced the living room floor. The next day, my nephew's father and I went to see his Lawyer. We wanted to know what he was facing, who was testifying and what his chances of winning the case were. After a few court status hearings, my nephew beat the murder charge. We all were happy to see him walk out of that courtroom.

I was over at my parent's house, and the phone rang.

I picked it up and a familiar female voice said "Where you been? I've been trying to catch you for over a year but your parents said you didn't stay there anymore, but you come over from time to time."

The girl on the other line was Rihanna. She said that she needed to talk to me.

"I'll be over in 30 minutes. Don't go anywhere," She said.

I waited on the front porch until she got there. She was driving an old model two-door car. I walked out of the house to the car and got in. She didn't look the same anymore. She had gained a lot of weight, estimated to be 270 lbs. She had a cigarette in her mouth, puffing like her nerves had gotten the best of her. She had cut her hair short, giving off a lesbian look. She said that she needed someone who could go up inside the gun store on St. Barnaby Rd. and purchase the guns at a cheaper price. The gun store owner was supposed to sell the guns at a cheaper price, but we still needed to go through the regular formalities of getting a background check.

I told her, "You must be crazy! I'm not going to a gun store, using my name."

She said, "No! You got to use another name."

I asked her, "How will I do that?"

She said, "Just get someone's birth Certificate, and Social

Security card."

I said, "Who?"

She asked me, "What's up with that guy that I saw over your house that day? He looked slow enough to go for fried ice cream."

I said, "No, find someone else."

She plotted on getting the info from someone. She called me again at my parent's home. She said that she had an ID with a dummy company on it. Rihanna had some Africans she introduced me to, who had an electronic business downtown on F St. NW. We all walked down to the basement of the store. They had me take a picture and created a false ID that could match a $746.36 check. The name that was on the check looked to be a male from another country. I didn't know how Rihanna came across this check. She was always scheming then she took a photo for the next plot.

A few days later, she came past my parent's house while a guy I knew was there. I let her talk to the guy and from paying attention to her talk, she could've been a good used car saleswoman, because she persuaded him out of all his identification. She showed him an ID with the fictitious company, under another false last name, with her correct first name that made it seem more real, what she was saying. She said the company was going to log his info down, through his social security and birth certificate. The look on her face was serious like she was sincere.

We took his social security card and birth certificate and made a duplicate. I gave him back his credentials and said that the female said they would call him. I went downtown to the motor vehicle and took my learner's permit.

Then I took the driver's test. All in Washington D.C. I switched the D.C. license over to a Maryland driver's license then I was able to walk into the gun store in Maryland and purchase a firearm. In D.C. there are no gun stores because firearms are illegal unless you're licensed as some type of law enforcement. I had to wait two weeks for clearance. The gun owner also was crooked, so he was giving me deals.

Rihanna had her own line of customers. I had lost a lot of my clientele because I'd been away and some of my past customers were gone. Since our last encounter, she had been in all types of schemes. She was doing checks, credit cards, selling marijuana, and now guns again but I still had it in the back of my mind that she burnt me before, so I had to watch her. I had promised myself that I wasn't going to indulge in any illegal activities again, but I needed the money to pay my bills and provide for my son. One thing I never touched again in life was narcotics.

A lot of the older guys my age didn't like Lil Rom. They felt he was into too much unnecessary drama but they dealt with him because they liked me, and they knew I liked Rom. I had been knowing him since he was only 5 years old, through his cousin.

Rom and I went to this club in Rivertown, Md. Rom was a fly dresser. He was driving a red 93' 300ZX.

He said, "Damn man, a lot of guys we knew have been dead a while now," like he was thinking about his own life. "I don't want to go out like Chi, Daryl, Tim, Keith, Chuck and a lot of other guys we knew."

I told him, "That's rough man."

He told me that he just claimed his Shahada, the first pillar of Islam. Even though he came up in a devoted Christian home.

I told him, "Muslim! You came up in church."

"But I feel Islam more than Christianity," he said.

164

A Fork in the Road

I told him, "Whatever makes you happy man."

I had just got two bulletproof vests, a dirt ball cheap from another source, and a Street sweeper that carried 12-gauge shells. I sold them for a good price. I was waiting for Rom to come past my apartment, so we could go out to Chesapeake Bay Seafood house. He said that he was stopping past a female's spot first, then he was heading my way.

I waited and waited for him to come by until it started getting late. I fell asleep. I got a call from Black that he heard Rom got killed.

I said, "That's impossible," I had talked to him a few hours ago. The next day, I called his grandmother's phone.

I said, "How are you doing Mam, is Rom home?"

She said, "Who's this?"

I said, "George."

She said, "I'm sorry to announce George, that Rom got killed late yesterday evening."

I went numb. I couldn't believe it. Someone killed my man.

He was found in the alley, lying beside his car, body

165

riddled up. The shooter even blew his face off, so it could be a closed casket.

I went to his wake. I had to sit down before walking even closer because his death really hit me hard. A hit was put on him by the guys I hoped would spare him because I liked him but I guess that wasn't enough. But what made it so bad was that they tried to see if I knew who'd killed him. The guy paid another young guy a chop shop vehicle to kill him.

I found out through a female, who was talking because she was in the area when he got killed. When she described the guys who she saw standing near the bus stop like they were catching a bus, I automatically knew who was behind it. These guys don't catch no fucking bus. They have cars but they were actually putting their play into action.

One of the guys is a very close friend of mine like a brother, and he was behind it also. I felt like Jimmy when Tommy got killed on "GoodFellas."

There wasn't much I could do, because Tommy was a hothead. The same with Rom. They felt he was a loose wire that needed to be fixed.

I had gotten so paranoid that I thought I was next to get

killed. When I was around any of my friends, I always kept a pistol on me, thinking they were trying to trick me into getting killed. I had gotten so paranoid that I hired my own personal barber to come by the house to cut my hair because I didn't trust those barbershops. I'd seen a few guys get knocked off while sitting in the chair and even while I was getting my haircut at home, I still kept a .38 in the cabinet just in case the barber was on some bullshit. It doesn't cost much to have someone killed in the hood.

I went past Rihanna's apartment because she called me over to her new place. When I got over there, a female let me inside. Also, it was another female in the apartment sitting on the couch watching television with a little boy, who I think was her son. I asked where Rihanna was. She said that she was in the room.

I walked to the room and lightly knocked. I opened the room door. Rihanna was in the bedroom watching some porn, while another female's face was buried in between her legs. She had a blunt of marijuana burning in the ashtray. She looked at me with a devilish grin and grabbed the blunt while resting her other hand on the girl's head. Rihanna had a boyfriend who was gullible, but she liked the fact that he'd spend his hardworking paycheck on her.

She called me because she wanted to see the gun receipts for all the guns I purchased. I stayed for 30 minutes and left. She eventually got me caught up again between two rival street crews that were beefing. She beat me and made it look like I had beat them then she disappeared and moved again.

The guys were sweating me hard about their money, or delivering what they had paid for. I was between a rock and a hard place. I felt like danger was closing in on me from all angles.

One day on a chilly December evening, Rihanna showed up unexpectedly while I was talking to Jarvis. He was washing his red Cadillac. She pulled up in a tinted window caravan with two other guys inside. She got out, wearing a fitted dress and open-toe heels. She had a coyish look on her face. I was surprised to see her pop up after what she did. I told her, she put me in a bad situation again. She told me to don't worry about it, she'll take care of it. She said that I worry too much. She pulled out a cigarette and lit it up. The smoke was dancing around my nose and mouth, causing me to choke. I told her she was being disrespectful by smoking in my face. I could see the guys in the caravan laughing at her disrespect.

A Fork in the Road

Jarvis stopped washing his car, trying to hear what was being said, because he knew she had run off with the guy's money. Rihanna took a long pull on the cigarette, causing her cheeks to fill with smoke. She gave me a seductive look, then blew the smoke in my face. The two guys in the caravan burst out laughing. I closed my eyes and took the blow from the cigarette smoke.

When I opened my eyes, she had a smile on her face and started walking back to her vehicle. The smoke in my face was a "Fuck you" gesture. I turned towards Jarvis who was furious from what he just witnessed then his frown turned into a smile, locking eyes with mine. We both were reading each other's minds. Then we both started laughing when she drove off. Two weeks later she was found shot in the head, and her so-called bodyguard was shot two times in the head and one in the jaw.

Chapter 22

> "I Shall never repeat such a mistake:
> I Shall never fall into such a trap again."
>
> **—Yoruba Proverb**

In 1994, the detectives started investigating the case. They first started questioning people about Jarvis. Then about 4 days later, the Homicide detectives and regular Metropolitan police raided my parent's house looking for me. Then they later raided the resident out of Prince George's County and arrested me around 11 am. They kept me in a small room for 6 hours, handcuffed behind my back until my arms were numb, even though I had a cast on my hand from an injury. The room had only one bright light above, and a metal stool. There were no toilets or sinks. I held my urine for hours. It was a small slot on the door that the police opened every 2 hours and asked me my name. After I stated my name, they would close the slot and repeat the same procedure every 2 hours.

When they finally let me out of the room, still handcuffed, they walked me into the interrogation room. They interrogated me for two straight hours. They wouldn't let me make a phone call or nothing. They played the good cop, bad cop. Then they sent me to the Upper Marlboro Correctional Center until the US Marshals came to extradite me back to Washington, DC. The US Marshals didn't extradite me back to Washington, DC, until 4 days later.

I was sent to DC Jail and later scheduled for a line-up. The first line-up witness didn't show up. In the second scheduled line-up, the witness didn't pick me out. Then they scheduled a Photo Array in which I was picture number 4. The witness picked number 7. The detectives called the guy weeks later and had him look at the photo array again. This time the witness supposedly chose my photo. I was indicted in March 1995. The Detectives found in Rihanna's phone book and personal papers the evidence linking me to running guns and false IDs.

My Attorney said she was under investigation and the FBI was about to stage a raid on the day she and the guy was shot.

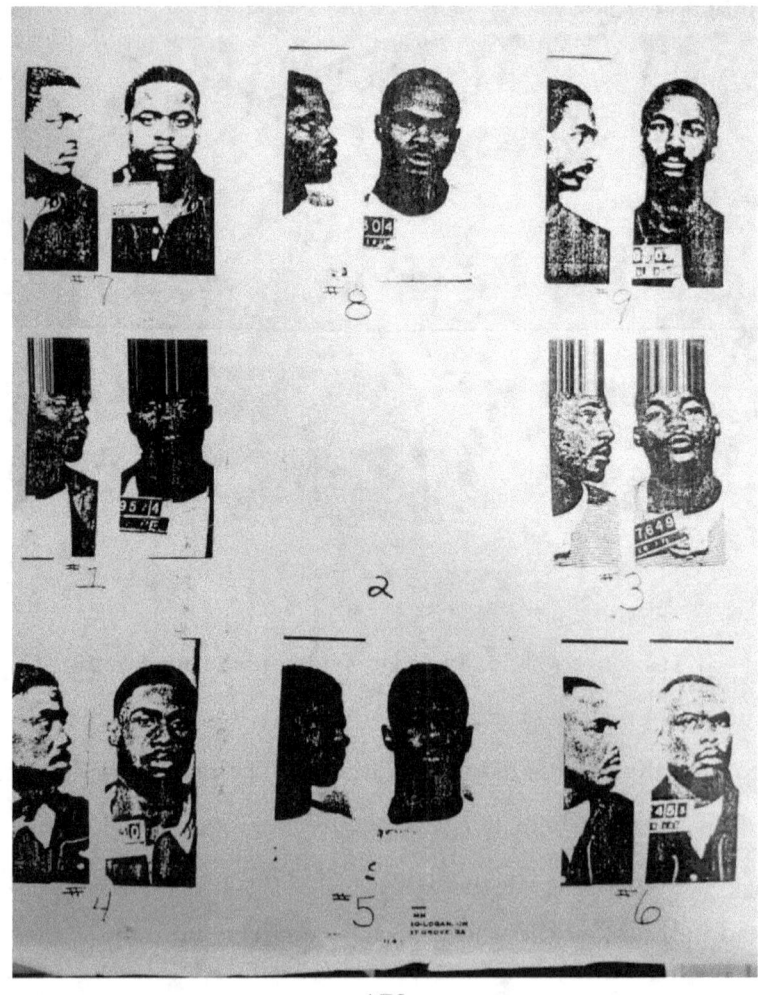

A Fork in the Road

I had these Public Defenders at first chopping at me to plead out. I wasn't going to plead. The prosecutor offered a 15-year plea. I told my attorney that I wasn't pleading for anything. I later hired a paid Attorney. My new Attorney said that the victims were reported having several altercations with other individuals. We went to trial in December 1995. My trial went on for two weeks. The jurors deliberated for 2 days, before coming back with a verdict. The jurors found me guilty on a 4-count indictment. Each count carries a term of life. I was numb from the verdict but I didn't show my disappointment. I maintain my composure.

I was transported back to DC jail after the verdict. It was the day before Christmas Eve. I sat on my bunk gazing into thought. The next day, I was called for a visit. My brother Bay came to see me. He was high, but he still made it down to see his brother.

He said "I never wanted this life for you. I wish you would have gone to college and been a doctor or something."

Nodding in between the silence of our visit. My brother said "Take Care, Lil brother, I'll be back to see you again."

When he stood up, I could see his eyes looking glossy.

173

I said "Okay, bro. Take care of yourself, I'm ok."

My brother walked to the booth, letting the guards know he was leaving. I went back to the unit and called home. My father answered the phone.

"Hey Son, how are you holding up?"

"I'm okay Dad," I replied.

"I wished we had sent you off to military school like we intended." said my father. His voice was sounding like he was hoarse.

"Everything will work itself out," I told my dad to ease his worries.

"We love you son," he said.

"I love you all too," I replied and then we both hung up.

A week later, I called home and my mother's voice sounded sad, and low, in which I could barely hear her, due to the loud noise in the jail. The inmates in Jail are always yelling when they talk.

I asked my mother if everything was Okay.

She said, "No, your father passed away this morning in his sleep."

A Fork in the Road

The guards were calling for lockdown at the same time I received the news. I told my mother that I was going to call her back. I went to my cell and gazed into thought of the days when I was a child, spending those precious moments with my family. Those times with my father, fixing my bike and throwing the football in the alley.

February 13, 1996, was the day of my sentencing. I was sentenced to 51 years to Life.

On March 6th, I was shipped off to Lorton, Va. to serve my time.

I thought about a statement that Paul Castellano said, before being murdered:

"This Life we live is a good life, the money, fortune and respect. But it's so many ways to screw it up."

My childhood friend, Mike— R.I.P.

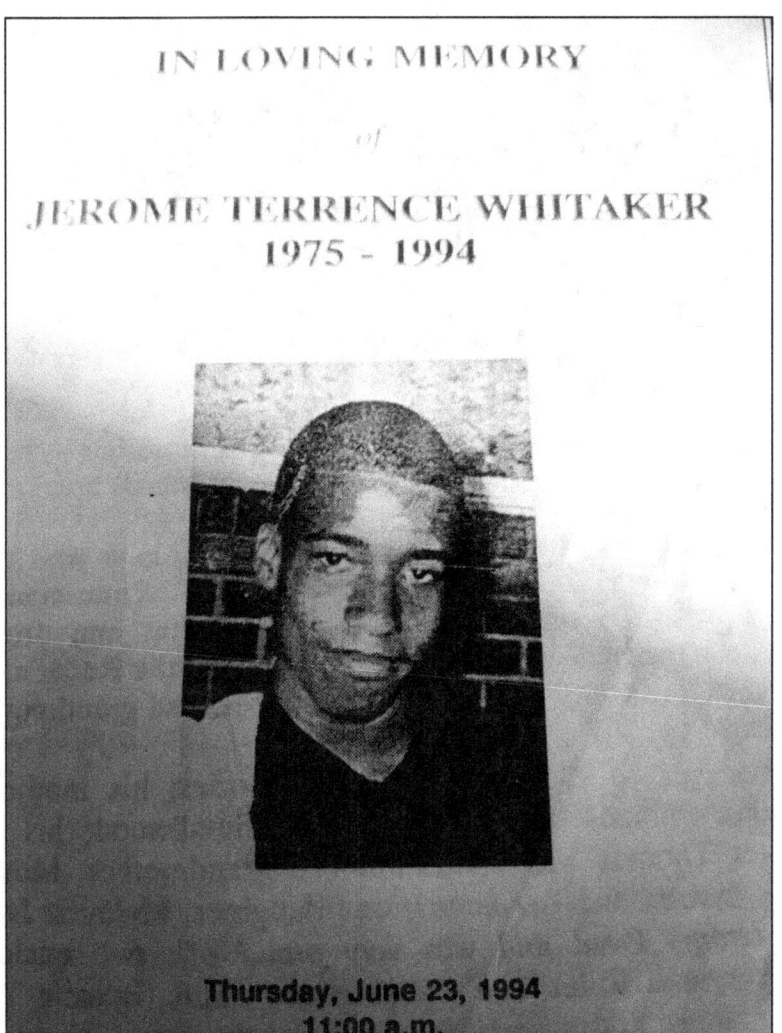

IN LOVING MEMORY

of

JEROME TERRENCE WHITAKER
1975 - 1994

Thursday, June 23, 1994
11:00 a.m.

My childhood friend, Rome— R.I.P.

R.I.P.